Mathematics for ESL Learners

Janet C. Arrowood

ScarecrowEducation
Lanham, Maryland • Toronto • Oxford
2004

Published in the United States of America
by ScarecrowEducation
An imprint of The Rowman & Littlefield Publishing Group, Inc.
4501 Forbes Boulevard, Suite 200, Lanham, Maryland 20706
www.scarecroweducation.com

PO Box 317
Oxford
OX2 9RU, UK

British Library Cataloguing in Publication Information Available

Library of Congress Cataloging-in-Publication Data

Arrowood, Janet C.
Mathematics for ESL learners / Janet C. Arrowood.
p. cm.
ISBN 1-57886-155-1 (pbk. : alk. paper)
1. Mathematics—Study and teaching. 2. English language—Textbooks for foreign speakers. I. Title.
QA11.2.A77 2004
510′.71—dc22

2004005767

∞ ™ The paper used in this publication meets the minimum requirements of American National Standard for Information Sciences—Permanence of Paper for Printed Library Materials, ANSI/NISO Z39.48-1992. Manufactured in the United States of America.

Contents

Introduction

Why should learning mathematics be part of English as a Second Language (ESL) studies? Because you use mathematics everyday, and the systems in America have many differences from the systems in your home country.

There are thousands of mathematics books available. Some are practical, some are theoretical, and some are technical. But none of these books was developed with the intent of helping ESL learners adapt (get used to) to day-to-day living in a strange new land.

Mathematics for ESL Learners will help you with several important things. First, it will help you improve your mathematical and reasoning skills. It provides the means to "brush up on" and refresh (review) the applied mathematics skills you learned in the past. But this book goes much farther than just helping you refresh your memory. It provides real-world skills to help you function (live) in this country.

Second, you have to make a major transition when you live in America. You have to learn to use and understand the American Standard Measurement (ASM) system. The ASM system is very different from the metric system you probably grew up with. At the same time, many measurements are similar in value. In that sense, learning the ASM system is like learning a new language. The concepts and values are similar. Only the words are different. Finally, you need to learn to make the connection between the new language you are learning and using, and the everyday use of practical mathematics.

What is "practical mathematics"? It is the application of numbers and concepts to everyday living. You need to understand (know) ASM to function in American society. You need to earn a living, pay taxes, pay bills, save money, budget, shop for food and other items, go on vacations, read maps, cook, estimate costs, and much more. And you have to do it in a new (different) country with an unfamiliar (strange, unusual) way of measuring things.

In this book, you're going to find lots of charts to help you make ASM and metric conversions. You're going to learn how to make a budget, how to estimate costs, and how to use mathematics to make your life easier. You're also going to apply many concepts and words you've been learning in your ESL or other English classes. Best of all, you will have a reference book you can use when you need to convert something or figure something out.

We've also included a glossary at the end of the book so you can look up (find) unfamiliar words and phrases. To help your vocabulary and understanding of American English, this book has alternate words in parentheses (brackets) after similar words. For example, an alternate word for "fuel" is "gas," so you'll see this in a paragraph. When you fill your car with gas (also called "fuel"), you need to know the pump works in gallons, not liters! Since there is a bit less than 4 liters in 1 gallon, you'll put in too much fuel (gas) if you think you should not stop filling the tank when the pump shows 25! Because the pump works in gallons, that would be close to 100 liters. You would have fuel spilling (pouring out) on the ground (parking lot).

OVERVIEW

Why take a course in mathematics just for learners of English as a Second Language (ESL)? You probably are already studying ESL or have already taken English classes, so why should mathematics be a special subject?

There are many things you need to know to live comfortably in America. Many things are different from your home country. Some of you will only live here for a few years while you attend college or graduate school. Many of you have already moved here and plan to stay. In either case, life is very different here. Numbers and mathematics play a big role in America.

As you adjust to life in the United States, you need to learn to plan how you will spend money. This is called making a budget. You need to be able to work with ASM instead of metric measurements. You need to know how to use maps to find places. You need to become familiar with American ways of writing decimals, large numbers, and mathematical symbols. You need to become comfortable (at ease) with American ways and expressions (phrases, idiom, sayings). Most important, you need to learn and understand that Americans have many different ways to say the same thing.

American English has many words with meanings that are very close (similar). This is not the case in many languages. You may only have two or three ways to say something. Nowhere are the choices more obvious (apparent) than in mathematical concepts. For example, see table I.1.

Think about it. See if you can think of several more words or phrases whose meanings are similar to the ones in table I.1. As you can see (tell), we have a lot of ways to say the same thing!

Living in America means learning the "ins and outs" or customs of another culture. Mathematics is about money, and culture is about money, so mathematics and culture are related. If you need to buy a car and you want to take out a loan (by borrowing money), you use applied mathematics to decide if you can afford (manage) the loan payments. If you want a credit card, you need to make sure you can pay the bill (charges) each month. That means you need a budget so you don't spend more money than you earn. When you have a job, you pay taxes. Taxes are a percentage of your income, and they are another application (use) of mathematics in your life in America.

Even things that seem simple, like (such as) telling time and writing dates, are probably done differently here than in your home country. If

Table I.1 Meter and Yard Comparisons

If you want to compare 1 meter and 1 yard, you can do so in many ways. You can say:

1. One meter is about the same as 1 yard.
2. One meter is a bit longer than 1 yard.
3. One yard is a bit shorter than 1 meter.
4. One meter is 10% longer than 1 yard.
5. One yard is 11% shorter than 1 meter.
6. A meter and a yard are very similar in length.
7. A meter and a yard are about the same distance.
8. Meters and yards can be substituted for each other.
9. One meter is 1.1 yards.

you don't realize how things are different here, you might miss your plane. You might go to a concert on the wrong day. You might pay your bills too late (past due) or too early (too soon).

If you write numbers with commas for decimals and periods for large numbers, that is opposite to how Americans do it. If you see a number like 1.000 and think, "That's one thousand," you are in for a surprise. In the United States 1.000 would be one (1), not one thousand, because we write 1.000 as 1,000. Also, we write 1,80 as 1.80.

Many things you do every day are based on the relationships between numbers—mathematics. When you plan to drive somewhere, you use mathematics for many things. You need to have a budget for hotels or campgrounds (caravan parks), food or restaurant meals, gasoline (fuel), highway tolls (user fees), sightseeing, emergencies, souvenirs, and other things. You will need maps, and you will need to be able to read (understand) those maps. There is a lot of information on a map. When you know a few standard things, maps are easy to read. You can tell how far it is (in miles) between cities, how far it is to your highway exit (where you leave the highway), and much more.

When you look (apply) for a job, you need to know how much the job pays in salary or hourly wage. You also need to know how much money you need to live on (pay your expenses). That's part of your budget. Then you need to know how much of your total income (earnings) you must pay in taxes. When you subtract the taxes you pay (owe) from the amount your job pays, that is your "take-home pay"—the amount of money you can spend (live on). If your take-home pay is the same or more than your budget, great. If your take-home pay is less than your budget, you need a new job, a second job, or a smaller budget.

1

Conversions and Basic Mathematical Concepts

Practical mathematics (math), is often called applied math. This type of math is used on a daily basis. As an ESL student, you also have to learn to live in a new culture. You probably came from a country that uses the metric system. In America, we still use American Standard Measurement, or ASM. It is similar to the system still used sometimes in the United Kingdom.

If you are using this book, English is probably not your first language. This means that you are learning concepts, words, and phrases that may not exist in your native language. English is a "hybrid" language: It is composed of words that came from many different languages. As a result, English has many ways to say one thing, and each way (word or phrase) has a slightly different meaning. You also have to learn a system of measuring things that is used almost nowhere else in the world!

You probably learned British English if you studied English in your home country. There are many differences in word usage between British and American English. There are also differences in the spelling of many words. This book is written in American English. The United Kingdom is transitioning (changing) to the metric system; America is not. In America, you will see the metric system in scientific applications, but rarely in everyday situations.

In this chapter, you will learn to convert between ASM and metric systems, and between metric and ASM systems. You will also learn many concepts such as:

- About
- Almost
- Nearly

- Close to
- A bit more than
- A bit less than
- Approximately

and so forth. Math is a good tool for learning these concepts since many metric measurements are close to (similar to) certain ASM measurements. The glossary at the end of this book lists and explains many of these new terms for you.

1.1 BASIC CONVERSIONS: ASM TO AND FROM METRIC

Let's start with the metric measurements and units you use every day. We will compare them to their ASM counterparts—the ASM units that are closest to metric measurements.

Tables 1.1 through 1.4 are useful references. They are also repeated in appendix A.

It is very useful to know approximate (nearly the same as) conversions. For example, one (1) meter is longer than one (1) yard. But it is not much longer. It is only about 10% longer. One yard is about 10% shorter than 1 meter. When you are trying to figure out how far 100 yards is, it is good to know it is about 100 meters. Actually, 100 yards is about 10% shorter (that is, less distance) than 100 meters. More specifically, 100 yards is about 90 meters. Since 100 meters is about 10% more than 100 yards, 100 meters is about (almost the same as) 110 yards.

The lines in figure 1.1 show you the relative lengths of 1 meter and 1 yard. The 2 lines are drawn to scale. That means the relationship between them is precise. If the page were wide enough, and you lengthened (increased) each line by the same percentage, they would be 36 inches (1 yard) and 39.37 inches (1 meter) long.

As you can see, there is not a lot of difference between the two lines! Understanding the relationship between 1 yard and 1 meter is an easy first step to working with ASM.

Table 1.1 Basic Conversions

Distance/Height/Length Conversions and Abbreviations	
Unit of Measurement Distance, Height, and Length	*Conversions/Comparisons*
1 inch (in.) is about	2.5 centimeters (cm) (British: centimetres).
1 centimeter (cm) is about	0.4 inches (in.).
1 foot (ft.) is about	30 centimeters (cm).
1 yard (yd.) is a bit smaller than	1 meter (m) (British: metre).
1 meter is a bit bigger than	1 yard (yd.).
1 yard (yd.) is exactly	3 feet (ft.).
1 meter (m) is a bit more than	3 feet (ft.).
1 hectare is about	2.5 acres (ac.).
1 acre (ac.) is about	0.4 hectares.
1 mile (mi.) is a bit less than	2 kilometers (km) (British: kilometres).
2 kilometers (km) are a bit more than	1 mile (mi.).
1 half (1/2 or 0.5) mile (mi.) is a bit less than	2 kilometer (km).
1 mile (mi.) is exactly	5,280 feet (ft.).
1 mile is about	1,600 meters (m).
6 miles (mi.) is about	10 kilometers (km).
10 kilometers (km) is about	6 miles (mi.).

1.1.1 Practice Exercises

Here are some conversions for you to try. In the first set, you need to fill in the blank with a word or phrase such as "about the same as," "close to," or other suitable (appropriate, correct) term. Your goal is to pick (choose) a word or phrase (several words) that explains the relationship between ASM and metric measurements. There can be more than one correct word or phrase to choose from. The tables in section 1.1 should help you find the answers.

For example:

- 1 yard is ________ 1 meter. One possible correct answer: 1 yard is *a bit shorter than* 1 meter. Another possible correct answer: 1 yard is *almost the same as* 1 meter.

In the second set of exercises, you need to fill in the correct metric or ASM measurement.

Table 1.2 Basic Conversions

Weight/Dry Measures
Conversions and Abbreviations

Unit of Measurement Weight/Dry Measures	*Conversions/Comparisons*
1 ounce (oz.) is about	28 grams (g).
30 grams (g) is a bit more than	1 ounce (oz.).
4 ounces (oz.) is a bit more than	100 grams (g).
4 ounces (oz.) is exactly	1/4 of 1 pound (lb.).
100 grams (g) is a bit less than	4 ounces (oz.) or 1/4 of 1 pound (lb.).
8 ounces (oz.) is a bit less than	250 grams (g).
8 ounces (oz.) is exactly	1/2 of 1 pound (lb.).
250 grams (g) is a bit more than	1/2 of 1 pound (lb.) or 8 ounces (oz.).
16 ounces (oz.) is a bit less than	500 grams (g).
16 ounces (oz.) is exactly	1 pound (lb.).
1 pound (lb.) is a bit less than	1/2 of 1 kilogram (kg) or 500 grams (g).
1 kilogram (kg) is about	2.2 pounds (lbs.).
2 pounds (lbs.) is a bit less than	1 kilogram (kg).
100 pounds (lbs.) is about	45 kilograms (kg).
50 kilograms (kg) is about	110 pounds (lbs.).
220 pounds (lbs.) is about	100 kilograms (kg).
100 kilograms (kg) is about	220 pounds (lbs.).
1 metric ton (t) (also called "tonne") is about	2,200 pounds (lbs.).
1 AMS ton (t) is about	900 kilograms (kg).

For example:

- 1 inch is about the same as ________. Answer: 1 inch is about the same as 2.54 cm. (2.5 cm is also acceptable as an answer.)

Fill in the blank with a word or phrase:

a. 1 meter is ______________________________ 1 yard.
b. 50 liters is ______________________________ 13 gallons.
c. 30 cm is ______________________________ 1 foot.
d. 1 liter is ______________________________ 1 quart.

Answers:

a. Almost the same as; about the same as; similar to; nearly the same as; a bit longer than; 10% longer than. There are many possible (correct) answers.

Table 1.3 Basic Conversions

Volume/Liquid Measures
Conversions and Abbreviations

Unit of Measurement Volume/Liquid Measures	*Conversions/Comparisons*
1 ounce (oz.) is about	30 milliliters (ml).
30 milliliters (ml) is about	1 ounce (oz.).
8 ounces (oz.) is a bit less than	250 milliliters (ml).
8 ounces (oz.) is exactly	1 cup (c.).
1 cup (c.) is a bit less than	250 milliliters (ml).
16 ounces (oz.) is a bit less than	500 milliliters (ml) or 1/2 liter (l).
16 ounces (oz.) is exactly	2 cups (c.) or 1 pint (pt.).
2 cups (c.) is exactly	1 pint (pt.).
1 pint (pt.) or 2 cups (c.) is about	500 milliliters (ml) or 1/2 liter (l).
32 ounces (oz.) is a bit less than	1,000 milliliters (ml) or 1 liter (l).
32 ounces (oz.) is exactly	1 quart (qt.) or 2 pints (pts.).
1 quart (qt.) is a bit less than	1 liter (l).
64 ounces (oz.) is a bit less than	2 liters (l).
64 ounces (oz.) is exactly	1/2 gallon (gal.) or 2 quarts (qts.) or 4 pints (pts.) or 8 cups (c.).
1 gallon (gal.) is less than	4 liters (l).
13 gallons (gal.) is about	50 liters (l).
50 liters (l) is about	13 gallons (gal.).

Table 1.4 Basic Conversions

Temperatures
Conversions and Abbreviations

Unit of Measurement Temperatures	*Conversions/Comparisons*
0 degrees centigrade (also called Celsius) is exactly	32 degrees Fahrenheit.
32 degrees Fahrenheit is exactly	0 degrees centigrade.
10 degrees centigrade is about	50 degrees Fahrenheit.
50 degrees Fahrenheit is about	10 degrees centigrade.
20 degrees centigrade is about	68 degrees Fahrenheit.
68 degrees Fahrenheit is about	20 degrees centigrade.
25 degrees centigrade is about	75 degrees Fahrenheit.
75 degrees Fahrenheit is about	25 degrees centigrade.
28 degrees centigrade is about	82 degrees Fahrenheit.
82 degrees Fahrenheit is about	28 degrees centigrade.
−40 degrees Fahrenheit is exactly	−40 degrees centigrade.

Figure 1.1 Comparison: 1 Yard and 1 Meter

b. A bit more than; almost the same as; close to; nearly the same as. Again, there are many correct answers.
c. Almost exactly the same as; nearly the same as; a bit less than; very close to. Again, there are many right (correct) answers.
d. A bit more than; almost the same as; close to. As with the other examples, there are many possible (correct) answers.

Fill in the blank with the correct metric or ASM equivalent:

Note that to be "equivalent" means to be very close to the same (equal). So, if you see a metric measurement (value), you need to put in its ASM equivalent. If you see an ASM value (measurement), you need to put in the metric equivalent.

a. 30 grams (g) is a bit more than ___________.
b. 1 mile is a bit less than ___________.
c. 1 cup (c.) is a bit less than ___________.
d. 1 liter is a bit more than ___________
e. 28°C is almost the same as ___________.
f. 212°F is exactly the same as ___________.

Answers:

a. 1 ounce (oz.)
b. 2 kilometers
c. 250 grams
d. 1 quart
e. 82°F
f. 100°C

1.2 UNITS OF MEASUREMENT

When you want to say *how far* or *how close, how long, how heavy, how hot* or *how cold, how much*, or *how big* something is, you use "units of measurement." There are different types of "units of measurement":

1. Distance, height, width, length, and circumference (how far, how long, how big, and so forth)
2. Weights (called dry measures: how much, how heavy)
3. Volumes (called liquid measures: how much)
4. Temperatures (how hot or cold)

Tables 1.5 through 1.8 show you the closest equivalent units of measurement between the ASM and metric systems in distances, heights, widths, lengths, and circumference.

As we mentioned earlier, there are many abbreviations you will need to know. Americans rarely write things out in full when they can shorten the word or phrase by using an abbreviation. However, not all abbreviations make sense. Some, such as "lb." for pound, you just have to remember. In the metric system, you do not usually put a period after a measure-

Table 1.5 Closest Equivalent Measurements

Distance/Height/Length	
American Standard Measurements	*Metric Measurements*
No true counterpart	*millimeters* (also written as mm)
inches (abbreviated as in. or ")	*centimeters* (cm is the short form)
foot (singular), *feet* (plural) (both abbreviated as ft.)	No true counterpart
yard (abbreviated as yd.)	*meter* (short form is m)
mile (mi. is the short form)	*kilometer* (abbreviated km)

Table 1.6 Closest Equivalent Measurements

Weights/Dry Measurements	
American Standard Measurements	*Metric Measurements*
ounce (oz.)	gram (g)
pound (lb.)	kilogram (kg)
ton (t)	tonne (t)

Table 1.7 Closest Equivalent Measurements

Volumes/Liquid Measurements	
American Standard Measurements	*Metric Measurements*
teaspoon (tsp)	milliliter (ml)
tablespoon (tbs or tbsp)	milliliter (ml)
ounce (oz.)	No true counterpart
cup (c.)	No true counterpart
pint (pt.)	No true counterpart
quart (qt.)	liter (l)
gallon (gal.)	No true counterpart

Table 1.8 Closest Equivalent Measurements

Temperatures	
American Standard Measurements	*Metric Measurements*
Fahrenheit (F)	centigrade (or Celsius) (C)

ment's abbreviation. You also don't usually make the abbreviation plural when the measurement unit is plural (more than one). In ASM we use periods and make abbreviations plural in most cases. The main exception is foot and feet; "feet" is the plural of foot, but both are abbreviated ft. See sidebar 1.1 for more examples and exceptions.

For example:

a. Metric uses m for meter or meters. ASM uses yd. for 1 yard and yds. for 2 or more yards.
b. Metric uses km for kilometer or kilometers. ASM uses mi. for mile or miles. There is no plural for this abbreviation.

ASM Abbreviation Tips

If you don't use the period for ASM measurement abbreviations, it is okay. However, it is important to use plural abbreviations when appropriate (correct).

Sidebar 1.1

c. Metric uses l for liter or liters. ASM uses qt. for 1 quart and qts. for more than 1 quart.
d. The abbreviations for teaspoon (tsp) and tablespoon (tbs or tbsp) are not made plural when there are two or more teaspoons or tablespoons.

See table 1.9 for a full list of abbreviations.

1.3 MORE PRECISE CONVERSIONS: ASM TO AND FROM METRIC

You do not usually need to know exact conversions between AMS and metric values. Exact conversions are important if you are studying science, medicine, or engineering. To understand applied mathematics, you only need to know the approximate conversions. If you need more precise conversions, use the chart in table 1.10.

Table 1.11 has formulas (also called "formulae") to use when you need a precise conversion between ASM and metric values. The results are very close, but not close (near) enough for many engineering and scientific applications. If you need exact answers, consult an engineering or scientific textbook or manual.

Table 1.9 Table of Abbreviations and Odd Words

ounce = oz.	cup = c.
gram = g	tablespoon = tbs or tbsp
pound = lb.	teaspoon = tsp
kilogram = kg	yard = yd.
liter = l	meter = m
milliliter = ml	mile or miles = mi.
centimeter = cm	miles per hour = mph
ton (tonne) = t	millimeter = mm
quart = qt.	deciliter = dl
inch = in. (also written as ″)	pint = pt.
gallon = gal.	decimeter = dm
foot = ft. (singular)	kilometers per hour = kph
feet = ft. (plural) (also written as ′)	degrees Fahrenheit = °F
kilometer = km	degrees centigrade = °C

Table 1.10 More Precise Conversions to and from ASM/Metric

1 in. = 2.54 cm	1 cm = 0.4 in.	1 foot = 30 cm	25 cm = 10 in.
100 cm = 1 m	36 in. = 1 yd.	1 yd. = 0.915 m	1 m = 1.1 yd.
1 km = 1,000 m	1 mi. = 5,280 ft.	1 mi. = 1760 yds.	1 km = 0.62 mi.
1 mi. = 1.6 km	1 mi. = 1,600 m	2 km = 1.24 mi.	1 oz. = 28.3 g
28.3 g = 1 oz.	1 c. = 8 oz.	1 c. = 225 ml	250 ml = 1.125 c.
2 c. = 1 pt.	16 oz. = 1 pt.	1 pt. = 450 ml	500 ml = 17.4 oz.
1 qt. = 32 oz.	1 qt. = 2 pts.	1 qt. = 4 c.	1 qt. = 0.91 l
1 l = 1.1 qt.	1 l = 1,000 ml	1 qt. = 910 ml	1/2 gal. = 64 oz.
1/2 gal. = 2 qts.	1/2 gal. = 4 pts.	1/2 gal. = 8 c.	1/2 gal. = 1.83 l
2 l = 1.12 1/2 gal.	1/2 gal. = 1,830 ml	1 gal. = 128 oz.	1 gal. = 2.5 gal.
1 gal. = 4 qts.	1 gal. = 8 pts.	1 gal. = 16 c.	1 gal. = 3.7 l
4 l = 1.1 gal.	1 gal. = 3,760 ml	1 oz. = 28.3 g	4 oz. = 113.2 g
100 g = 3.5 oz.	8 oz. = 226.4 g	250 g = 9 oz.	16 oz. = 1 lb.
16 oz. = 454 g	500 g = 17.5 oz.	1 lb. = 0.454 kg	1 kg = 2.2 lbs.
2 lbs. = 0.9 kg	1 t = 2,000 lbs. (ASM)	1 t = 1,000 kg (metric)	0°C = 32°F (freezing point of water)
−40°C = −40°F	20°C = 68°F	25°C = 75°F	28°C = 82°F
100°C = 212°F (boiling point of water)	350°F = 176°C (common baking temperature)	400°F = 204°C (common baking temperature)	500°F = 260°C (common pizza-baking temperature)

1.4 BASIC CONCEPTS

Mathematics relies on (uses) many important basic concepts (ideas). Several of the most essential concepts are going to be discussed in the next several sections. These concepts are (1) using a number line to perform addition and subtraction; (2) performing mathematical operations in the correct order, using the Order of Operations; and (3) working with negative numbers.

1.4.1 Using the Number Line to Add and Subtract

You already know how to add and subtract. There is a way to make this process even easier—the number line. If you need to add or subtract negative numbers and positive numbers, the number line is a simple picture that makes the addition or subtraction much easier (see figure 1.2).

When you use a number line, you need to follow these steps:

1. Place a mark above the number line that is the same as (corresponds to) the first number in the equation. Note that the equation must only involve adding, subtracting, or both.

Table 1.11 Useful Conversion Formulas

To convert from Fahrenheit to centigrade:
- Subtract 32 from the temperature in °F.
- Divide the result by 9.
- Multiply the result by 5.

Example:
To convert 212°F to C:
- 212 − 32 = 180
- 180 ÷ 9 = 20
- 20 · 5 = 100°C

To convert from centigrade to Fahrenheit:
- Divide the temperature in °C by 5.
- Multiply the result by 9.
- Add 32 to the result.

Example:
To convert 28C to F:
- 28 ÷ 5 = 5.6
- 5.6 · 9 = 50.4
- 50.4 + 32 = 82.4 (Note how close this is to the approximate conversion in table 1.4.)

To convert from miles to kilometers, multiply the number of miles by 1.62.
Example:
200 mi. · 1.62 = 324 km

To convert from kilometers to miles, multiply the number of kilometers by 0.62.
Example:
200 km · 0.62 = 124 mi.

To convert from inches to centimeters, multiply the number in inches by 2.54.
Example:
50 in. · 2.54 = 127 cm

To convert from centimeters to inches, multiply the number in centimeters by 0.394.
Example:
100 cm · 0.394 = 39.4 in.

To convert from quarts to liters, multiply the number in quarts by 0.91.
Example:
4 qts. · 0.91 = 3.94 l

To convert from liters to quarts, multiply the number in liters by 1.1.
Example:
6 l · 1.1 = 6.6 qts.

To convert from liters to gallons, multiply the number in liters by 0.27.
Example:
4 l · 0.27 = 1.1 gal.

To convert from gallons to liters, multiply the number in gallons by 3.64.
Example:
4 gal. · 3.64 = 14.56 l

To convert from kilograms to pounds, multiply the number in kg by 2.2.
Example:
80 kg · 2.2 = 176 lbs.

To convert from pounds to kilograms, multiply the number in lbs. by 0.45.
Example:
150 lbs. · 0.45 = 67.5 kg

To convert from yards to meters, multiply the number in yards by 0.915.
Example:
5 yds. · 0.915 = 4.58 m

To convert from meters to yards, multiply the number in meters by 1.1.
Example:
10 m · 1.1 = 11 yds.

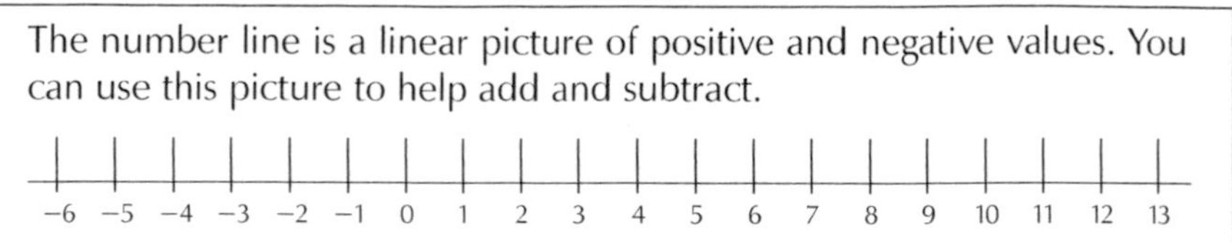

Figure 1.2 The Number Line

2. If the second number is *positive* and you are *adding* it to the first number, move to the *right* of the mark by the absolute value of the number. Place a mark at that point. If you are only adding two numbers, the second mark is above the number that is the answer to the equation. If you are adding or subtracting more numbers, you need to repeat the process.
3. If the second number is *negative* and you are *adding* it to the first number, move to the *left* of the mark by the absolute value of the number. Place a mark at that point. If you are only adding two numbers, the second mark is above the number that is the answer to the equation. If you are adding or subtracting more numbers, you need to repeat the process.
4. If the second number is *positive* and you are *subtracting* it from the first number, move to the *left* of the mark by the absolute value of the number. Place a mark at that point. If you are only adding two numbers, the second mark is above the number that is the answer to the equation. If you are adding or subtracting more numbers, you need to repeat the process.
5. If the second number is *negative* and you are *subtracting* it from the first number, move to the *right* of the mark by the absolute value of the number. Place a mark at that point. If you are only adding two numbers, the second mark is above the number that is the answer to the equation. If you are adding or subtracting more numbers, you need to repeat the process.

1.4.2 Order of Operations

The most important basic mathematical principle you need to understand is called the Order of Operations. Adding (increasing) and subtracting (taking away) are both mathematical "operations." In the case of addition, the order in which you perform (do) the operation is not important (relevant). If you are adding numbers where some are positive (greater than zero) and some are negative (less than zero), you can still do (perform) the addition in any order, as long as you pay attention to (watch carefully) any negative (minus) signs associated with any number. This process is explained in section 1.4.1, "Using Number Lines," and section 1.4.3, "Working with Negative Numbers."

When you are adding positive numbers, the process is simple (easy, straightforward), as shown in sections 1.4.1 and 1.4.3. The Commutative Property of Addition applies (see section 1.4.1).

When you are subtracting numbers, the order in which you perform subtraction (mathematical operations) is critical (very important). You cannot change the order of the numbers unless you perform some additional mathematical operations (also called "functions"). See section 1.4.1, "Using Number Lines," and section 1.4.3, "Working with Negative Numbers," to understand why this is so (why you cannot do this). When some or all of the numbers you are subtracting are negative numbers, the order in which you perform the operations matters greatly. There is no Commutative Property of Subtraction.

Working with Addition

In order to proceed, it is extremely (very) important for you to clearly (thoroughly, completely) understand (know) the Commutative Property of Addition (see figure 1.3).

- Positive numbers can be added in any order:

  If $A + B = C$, then $B + A = C$

- So, for any collection of positive numbers n: $n_1 + n_2 + n_3 + \ldots =$ $\ldots n_3 + n_2 + n_1$. The order of the numbers represented by n_1, n_2, and n_3 does not matter as long as all the numbers are positive.

Figure 1.3 Commutative Property of Addition

Adding Two or More Positive Numbers

When you add two numbers and both are positive, the process is straightforward (easy, simple). You combine the values of the 2 numbers and the result is always a *bigger* number than either of the first two numbers. If you are adding three or more positive numbers, the result is always *larger* (bigger) than any of the three individual numbers. The result is also bigger (larger) than if you added any two of the three positive numbers together. (See figure 1.4 for an example.)

Working with Subtraction

The number line is very useful when subtracting numbers. Adding negative numbers can also be viewed (treated, considered) as subtraction.

Properties of Subtraction

Subtraction is *not* commutative. The Order of Operations is critical. If you change the order of the numbers, your answer will change. As mentioned earlier, there is no Commutative Property of Subtraction.

If you subtract (take away) one positive number from another, the answer is less than the value of either number you are working (dealing) with.

If you are subtracting two or more positive numbers, you need to perform the subtraction in the order each operation appears in the equation. Remember, there is *no* Commutative Property of Subtraction. (See figure 1.5 for an example.)

When you are adding a positive and a negative number, you can treat it as a type of subtraction. (See figure 1.6 for an example.)

We've looked briefly at the concept of Order of Operations. Now let's look at why the Order of Operations is so important, and why you need to understand it in real life.

When you are adding numbers, the order in which you do so does not matter. If some of the numbers being added are not positive (that is, if they are negative, or less than zero), you must pay special attention to their negative signs. But the addition (combining) process is still the same. (See figure 1.7 for an example.)

When a + b = c (adding two positive numbers)
Example:

$$2 + 4 = 6$$

- The result (answer) must be larger than (greater than) either 2 or 4. (Note: Both 2 and 4 are positive numbers. You should assume that a number is positive if there is no minus (−) sign in front of it.)

When a + b + c = d (adding three positive numbers)
Example:

$$4 + 5 + 6 = 15$$

- The answer (result) must be greater than (larger than) either 4 + 5, or 5 + 6, or 6 + 4. (Note: Four, 5, and 6 are positive numbers.)

Adding three or more positive numbers where the numbers n are represented by a, b, c, d . . . : a + b + c + d + . . . = . . . d + c + b + a, where $n_1 = a$, $n_2 = b$, $n_3 = c$, $n_4 = d$, and so forth

- The answer is greater than (bigger than) the sum of any *n*-1 numbers:

$$a + b + c$$
$$b + c + d$$
$$c + d + a$$
$$d + a + b$$

Note that the Commutative Property of Addition allows you to reverse or rearrange (change) the order of any group of numbers being added. The resulting answer does not change. If you add

$$a + b + c$$

the answer is the same as when you add:

b + c + a or
a + c + b or
b + c + a or
a + c + b or
b + a + c or
c + b + a

So if you add $n_1 + n_2 + n_3 + n_4$, the result must be greater than adding any three of the four n values n_1, n_2, n_3, or n_4.

Figure 1.4 Adding Positive Numbers

Subtracting Two Positive Numbers

$$a - b = c$$

Example:

$$8 - 5 = 3$$

- The answer (result) must be less than the value of either 8 or 5. As with the addition example in figure 1.4, you should assume numbers are positive unless you are told otherwise.
- Note: If you subtracted 5 − 8, the answer would be negative. In this example, the answer would be −3 (negative 3). The result (answer) is less than either 8 or 5, so the principle (statement) in this section applies.

Subtracting Two or More Positive Numbers

$$a - b - c = d$$

- You must perform the mathematical operations in the order they appear (the order they are written). Unlike addition, you cannot simply change the order of the numbers and get the same answer. If you are going to change the order of the numbers, there are other actions you must take. These actions are covered in the next subsections.

Figure 1.5 Subtracting Two or More Positive Numbers

If you try to total (add) the numbers in the example we just looked at, you must be very careful of the negative nine (−9). Note that the negative sign and the 9 are enclosed (placed) inside parentheses (brackets). This is to make it completely clear that the minus sign (−) belongs to (with) the 9 and is not the same as a sign (symbol) for subtraction.

When you are adding numbers where some numbers have negative signs (values less than zero), the negative sign replaces the addition symbol. This makes the operation the same as subtracting the second (negative) number from the first (positive) number.

This is a good time to look at number lines again. It is usually easier (simpler) to use a number line when you are adding or subtracting negative numbers. Section 1.4.3 has more examples of adding and subtracting positive and negative numbers.

In the earlier example, $5 + (-9) + 20$ becomes $5 - 9 + 20$. Since

Adding a Positive and a Negative Number: A Variation of Subtraction

$$a + (-b) = c$$

Example:

$$6 + (-8)$$

- Adding a negative number to a positive number reduces (decreases) the value of the positive number. Look at the number line below and start from positive 6, then add negative 8 (-8) by counting eight spaces to the left (the negative direction):

- The answer:

$$6 + (-8) = -2$$

Figure 1.6 Adding a Positive and a Negative Number

If you add:

$$5 + 9 + 20$$

The answer (total, value) is 34. If you change the order and add 20 + 5 + 9, or if you add 5 + 20 + 9, or 9 + 5 + 20, or 20 + 9 +5, or 9 + 20 + 5, the answer (result) is still 34.

- If you change the positive (greater than zero) 9 to a negative (less than zero) 9 (written as -9), the expression becomes

$$5 + (-9) + 20$$

Figure 1.7 Order of Operations: Addition

there is a combination of addition and subtraction in the expression, the Commutative Property of Addition does not apply. You can only apply the Commutative Property of Addition when all the operations involve (use) addition. In an expression (or equation) where there is a mix of "operators" (signs such as $+$, $-$, $\times$, $\cdot$, $\div$, or /), you cannot change the Order of Operations.

Multiplication Considerations

If you are multiplying several numbers and there are no other mathematical operations involved, you can perform (do) the multiplication in any order you wish (want to). This is the Commutative Property of Multiplication. Figure 1.8 shows an example of the Commutative Property of Multiplication.

If there are any other mathematical operations involved, you must be very careful to perform (do) them in the correct order or you will not get the right (correct) answer.

If you have a combination of multiplication, addition, or subtraction operations, you must always do them in the order shown in Figure 1.9.

Figure 1.10 shows you the actual process to use to follow the rules for Order of Operations.

Figure 1.11 is yet another example of applying the rules of Order of Operations.

If you added another mathematical operation to the equation in figure 1.12, such as subtraction, the Order of Operations would matter greatly.

- If you are multiplying $a \times b \times c$, you can also do the multiplication in the order

$$a \times c \times b \text{ or}$$
$$c \times b \times a \text{ or}$$
$$b \times c \times a \text{ or}$$
$$b \times a \times c \text{ or}$$
$$c \times a \times b$$

- The same principle holds true for additional variables (numbers) added to the expression $a \times b \times c$ (or any of its variations).

Figure 1.8 Commutative Property of Multiplication

- Perform all operations inside parentheses (or brackets) first. This is called "clearing" the parentheses.
- Perform any multiplication.
- Perform any division.
- Perform any addition or subtraction.

Figure 1.9 Order of Operations: Combined Mathematical Operations

Example

Equation:

$$5 + 3(5 - 3) - 7(6 + 4) = ?$$

- First, "clear" the parentheses.
- In this example, you need to perform (do) the subtraction in the first set of parentheses and the addition in the second set. The equation becomes:

$$5 + 3(2) - 7(10) = ?$$

- Next, perform any multiplication and division operations. In this example, there are two multiplication operations to be done (performed). The equation becomes:

$$5 + 6 - 70 = ?$$

- Finally, perform any addition and subtraction operations. The final answer to this equation is:

$$11 - 70 = -59$$

- The answer is a negative number. You could also perform the subtraction by starting at positive 11 on the number line and counting 70 numbers to the left—the negative (minus) direction. You would end at minus 59.

Figure 1.10 Order of Operations: Combined Mathematical Operations

For example:

If one of the two people in the lawn-mowing example only wanted his or her lawn mowed 10 months a year (but still twice each month those 10 months), the equation would change. Figure 1.12 shows the results of applying (using) a new mowing schedule.

Let's create the modified (changed) equation applying the rules for adding, subtracting, and multiplying, which you just reviewed (learned).

You have to change the equation to reflect (show) that one of the lawns is not being mowed every month. It is still being mowed twice a month when it is mowed at all, but during some months the lawn is not mowed. This means you will have to make a change to the number of months for one lawn, but not for the other. Be careful. Figure 1.13 shows the changes you need to make to the information in figure 1.12 in order to get the correct result (answer).

- If you have told someone you will give them \$20 to mow your lawn, and your neighbor has said she will pay that person the same amount of money to mow her lawn, you have said:
- We will pay 2×20 dollars to have our lawns mowed. That is the same as 20×2. In both cases, the product (result of the multiplication) is \$40.
- If you and your neighbor both want your lawns mowed for \$20 each twice each month for the entire year, you have said:

"We want someone to mow our lawns. We will each pay \$20 each time. There are two of us. We each want our lawn mowed two times per month. We want this arrangement to last for 12 months (one year)."

- When you are thinking of starting a lawn-care (mowing) service and you want to know how much money you can earn, here is how you can calculate your possible (projected, expected) earnings:

\$20 per lawn, times (multiplied by) 2 people, times 2 mowings per month, times 12 months in 1 year. The equation (in words) for that mathematical calculation is:

$$\$20 \times 2 \text{ lawns} \times 2 \text{ mowings} \times 12 \text{ months} = \$960 \text{ per year}$$

- In pure (just, only) numbers, the equation for this word problem would be:

$$20 \times 2 \times 2 \times 12 = 960$$

- If you wrote this equation (in words) as 12 months per year, times \$20 per mowing, times 2 people, for 2 times each month, the equation in numbers would be:

$$12 \times 20 \times 2 \times 2 = 960$$

- The order of the multiplication does not matter.

Figure 1.11 Word Problem: Combined Mathematical Operations

• Mowing cost:	\$20
• Mowing frequency:	2 times per month
• Number of months to mow:	10 for one person, 12 for the other person
• Number of lawns:	2

Figure 1.12 Revised Word Problem: New Schedule

- New equation in words:
- Number of mowings per month (first customer), times mowing cost, times number of months to mow + Number of mowings per month (second customer), times mowing cost, times number of months to mow.
- New equation in numbers:

$$(2 \times 20 \times 10) + (2 \times 20 \times 12) = ?$$

- First step: Perform (do) the mathematical operations inside each set of parentheses.

$$2 \times 20 \times 10 = 400 \qquad 2 \times 20 \times 12 = 480$$

- Second step: Perform the addition.

$$400 + 480 = 880$$

- Result (Answer): You can expect to earn $880 with this revised lawn-care schedule.

Figure 1.13 New Mowing Equation in Words and Numbers

Another way to write this equation is:

$$(2 \times 20)\,(10 + 12)$$

In this case, you still need to perform the operations inside the parentheses (multiplication in the first set, addition in the second set), then multiply the result together. This equation (see figure 1.14) shows you how to use (apply) the distributive property of multiplication.

Any time you are thinking of starting a business, you need to be able to do these calculations to see if you can earn enough money to cover (meet, satisfy) your budget. Let's look at a real-world application. Figure 1.15 depicts (shows) a situation you could encounter at home.

What are "expressions" when you are working with mathematical terms? Take a look at sidebar 1.2, "Expressions."

$$(a + b)(c) = ab + ac$$

By extension, $(a + b)(c \times d) = a(c \times d) + b\,(c \times d)$.

Figure 1.14 Distributive Property of Multiplication

- You are going to give your child an allowance so she can pay for her own snacks, bus rides, clothes, and CDs. In order to get the full amount of her allowance, she must perform certain chores and look after her younger brother. If she does not perform a chore (task) or if she goes out with friends instead of looking after her brother, her allowance is reduced. Her allowance is \$25 per week, but she loses \$1 for each chore she does not do (perform, complete) and \$2 for each time she is supposed to stay with (babysit) her brother and does not do so. She also gets \$1 for each extra chore (task) she does.
- If she fails to babysit (stay with) her brother two weeks in a row, the \$2 deduction is doubled each time.
- If your daughter fails to do three chores this week and doesn't look after her brother two times when she agreed to do so, and next week she does two extra tasks (chores) but doesn't babysit three times when she said she would, how much should her allowance be each week?

A = allowance, week one
B = allowance, week two

- If you do not follow proper Order of Operations, and just go from left to right, here's what happens:

$$A = 25 - 3 \times 1 - 2 \times 2 = ?$$

- First step: $25 - 3 = 22$
- Second step: $22 \times 1 = 22$
- Third step: $22 - 2 = 20$
- Fourth step: $20 \times 2 = 40$

- If you simply perform the mathematical operations from left to right, your daughter will get a *larger* allowance than she is supposed to. She will be rewarded for *not* doing her chores and *not* babysitting when she agreed to. She is being given more than the agreed upon \$25 and she did not help you at home.
- This first equation does not clearly show the correct order to perform the addition, subtraction, and multiplication. The equation was not written properly to show the Order of Operations. Since you have multiplication, addition, and subtraction, you must be very careful.
- Tip: Apply logic to math. If your daughter did less than you both agreed to, you *know* her allowance should be less than the maximum (full) amount. The only way she could get more than the full amount (\$25) is if she did extra chores, plus all the chores she was supposed to do and all the babysitting she agreed to do. The only way she could get exactly \$25 is if she completed the full amount of tasks (chores)

she agreed she would do, and did all the babysitting she agreed she would do. Stop and think about what the answer should be (look like).

- Now let's rewrite the equation for your daughter's first week's allowance so she gets the correct amount. Remember, since we are subtracting, not adding, her allowance should be less than $25.

$$A = 25 - (3 \times 1) - (2 \times 2)$$

- First step: Multiply the numbers in each set of parentheses.

$$(3 \times 1) = 3 \; (2 \times 2) = 4$$

- Second step: Replace the numbers in the parentheses with the answers in the first step.

$$25 - 3 - 4 = ?$$

- Third step: Subtract (take away) 3 from 25, and then take away (subtract) 4 from the result (answer).

First part: $25 - 3 = 22$
Second part: $22 - 4 = 18$

- Answer: Your daughter should get $18 this week. The answer *looks right*. It is logical since she should not get the full $25 and in fact should get a lot (significantly) less. She certainly should not get $40 when she did not complete all her chores or other work!

Second Week:

- For the second week, remember that there is a penalty for two weeks in a row of *not* performing the agreed upon babysitting. Instead of losing $2 for each time she did not babysit, your daughter loses twice as much—2 × $2 per time.
- Now the equation for her allowance looks like this. It is structured (set up) to allow you to do the operations in the proper order.

$$B = 25 + (2 \times 1) - (2 \times 3 \times 2)$$

- First step: Multiply the numbers in each set of parentheses. Remember that you can multiply in any order, as long as that is the only mathematical operation you are doing (performing). Go back to the Commutative Property of Multiplication if you need to review this concept.
- Second step: Rewrite the equation.

$$25 + 2 - 12 = ?$$

- Third step: Combine the numbers (terms) from left to right.

$$25 + 2 = 27$$
$$27 - 12 = 15$$

- The answer is $15. Although your daughter did some extra chores, she is paying the penalty for not babysitting two weeks in a row. Logic should tell you (indicate, show) that her allowance will be even less than last week. She only did a few extra chores and skipped even more babysitting times. She also had to give up twice as much allowance the second week for each missed babysitting task.
- Tip: Since you are not as familiar with English as you might like (wish) to be, you want to be careful that you understand the numbers you are using. You also need to be clear about the order in which you combine numbers or you could lose money.

Figure 1.15 Real-World Application

"Expressions"

An "expression" is a mathematical term for numbers connected by "signs" (such as +, −, ×, ·, ÷, and /) but without an equal (=) sign. An "equation" is just like an expression, but it includes an equal sign. An equation can usually be solved; an expression cannot be solved.

Sidebar 1.2

1.4.3 Working with Negative Numbers

Negative numbers are a way of showing that something is being reduced, or decreased. The number line is a very effective (simple) way to work with negative numbers. When you are adding a negative number to another number, you are moving to the *left* along the number line from the first number (see sidebar 1.3).

When you are subtracting (taking away) a negative number from another number, you are making the first number bigger (see sidebar 1.4). This is easier to understand by looking at the number line and the Rule of Changing Signs. You also need to know part of the Rule of Absolute Value, which is shown in figure 1.16.

Figures 1.17 through 1.20 give you examples of how to use the Rule of Absolute Value. This rule makes adding negative numbers to positive or negative ones much easier (simpler).

Adding Negative Numbers

If one or more of the numbers being added is negative (has a negative sign), the process of adding the numbers is different. See section 1.4.3, "Working with Negative Numbers," and section 1.4.1, "Using the Number Line to Add and Subtract," to learn (understand) how to work with these negative numbers.

Sidebar 1.3

Subtracting Negative Numbers

If one or more of the numbers being subtracted is negative (has a negative sign), the process of subtracting the numbers is different. See section 1.4.3, "Working with Negative Numbers," and section 1.4.1, "Using the Number Line to Add and Subtract," to learn (understand) how to work with these negative numbers.

Sidebar 1.4

The absolute value of a negative number is the same number without the negative sign. Absolute value refers to the "relative" (apparent) difference or distance. For example, if you walk backwards (the other way) 10 steps, you have walked -10 (minus 10) steps. But in absolute (real) terms, you have still moved 10 steps. You just went in the opposite direction (backwards).

Figure 1.16 Rule of Absolute Value

This process can be made even simpler by using a number line, as the next two figures show.

Adding a Negative Number to a Positive Number

- This is the same as subtracting the negative number from the positive number. You drop (leave off, get rid of) the negative sign and replace the addition sign with a minus (subtractions) sign.

$$10 + (-7) = 10 - 7 = 3$$

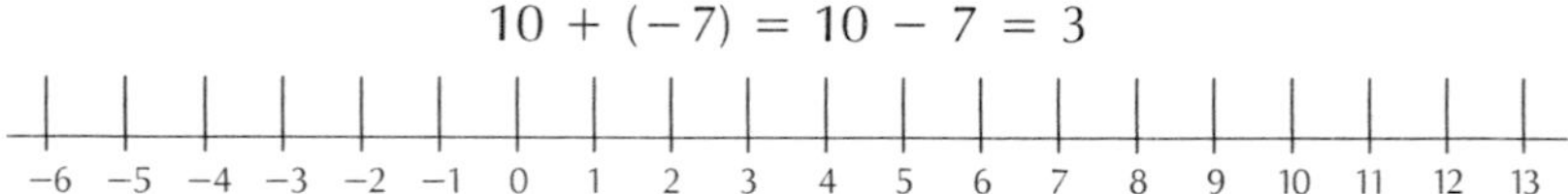

- The negative number reduces the value of the positive number. You move left beginning at the positive number on the number line by the number of spaces equal to the absolute value of the negative number.

Adding a Negative Number to a Negative Number

This is the same as adding the absolute value of both numbers and then replacing the negative sign. The first negative number becomes even more negative. On the number line, you start at the first negative number and move left by the absolute value of the second negative number.

$$-10 + (-7) = -(10 + 7) = -(17) = -17$$

−18 −17 −16 −15 −14 −13 −12 −11 −10 −9 −8 −7 −6 −5 −4 −3 −2 −1 0 1

- When there is a negative sign in front of a second or subsequent (additional) number in an equation, you put the number and the minus sign in brackets (parentheses) to show the minus sign "belongs" to the number. If you did not do this, you might subtract a number that should actually (really) be added.

Figure 1.17 Adding a Negative Number to Another Number

Subtracting a Negative Number from a Positive Number

- This is the same as adding the absolute value of the negative number to the positive number. You drop (leave off, get rid of) the negative sign and replace the minus sign with an addition (plus) sign.

$$10 - (-7) = 10 + 7 = 17$$

- The "negative" of a negative number increases the value of the positive number. You move right beginning at the positive number on the number line by the number of spaces equal to the absolute value of the negative number.

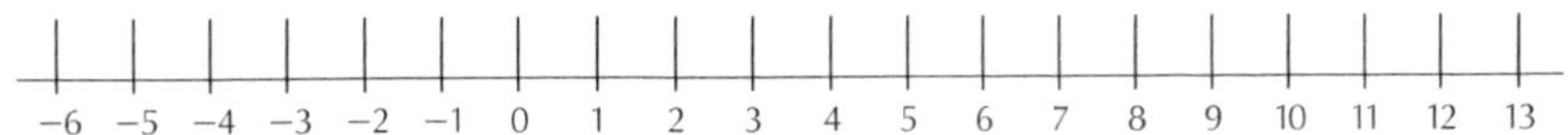

Subtracting a Negative Number from a Negative Number

- This is the same as adding the absolute value of the second negative number to the first negative number. You drop (leave off, get rid of) the negative sign and replace the minus sign with an addition (plus) sign. The first negative number becomes less negative. It may even become positive. On the number line, you start at the first negative number and move right by the absolute value of the second negative number.

$$-10 - (-7) = -10 + 7 = -3$$

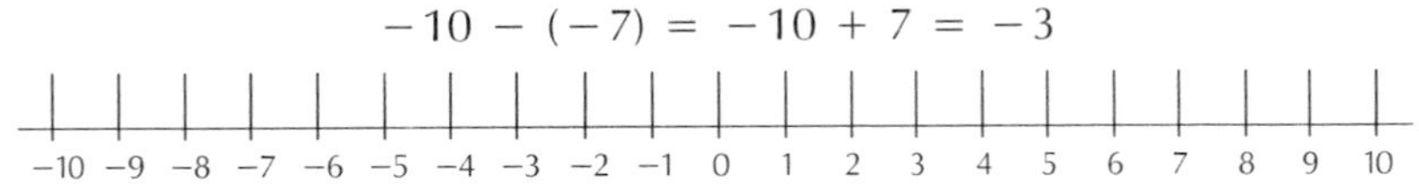

Figure 1.18 Subtracting a Negative Number from Another Number

Subtracting a Positive Number from a Positive Number

- When you are subtracting a positive number from a positive number, the first positive number becomes smaller. It may even become negative. On the number line, this subtraction operation is shown by starting at the first number and moving to the left by the value of the second number. You are taking something positive away from the first number, so the first number becomes smaller.
- Example:

$$12 - 6 = 6$$

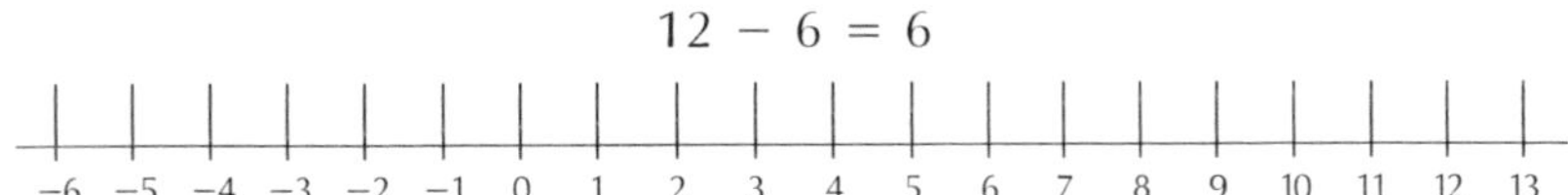

Subtracting a Negative Number from a Positive Number

- When you are subtracting a negative number from a positive number, change the negative sign to a positive (plus) sign and the subtraction (minus) sign to a plus sign. On the number line, this subtraction operation is shown by starting at the first number and moving to the right by the absolute value of the second number. You are taking something negative *away* from the first number, so the first number becomes larger.

- Example:

$$4 - (-3) = 4 + (+3) = 4 + 3 = 7$$

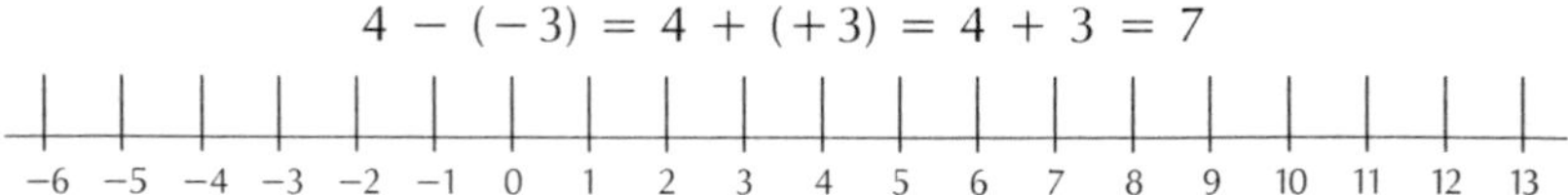

Subtracting a Positive Number from a Negative Number

- When you are subtracting a positive number from a negative number, change the subtraction sign to a plus (+) sign and make the second number negative. On the number line, this subtraction is shown by starting at the first (negative) number and moving to the left by the value of the second number. You are taking something positive away from the first number that is already negative, so the first number becomes even more negative (smaller).
- Example:

$$-1 - 5 = 1 - + (-5) = -6$$

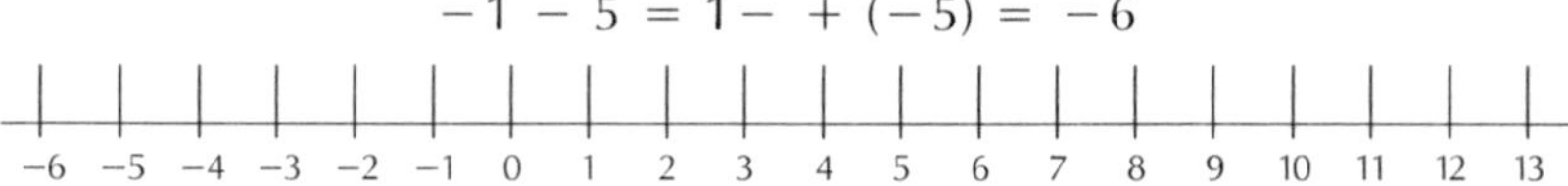

Subtracting a Negative Number from a Negative Number

- When you are subtracting a negative number from a negative number, change the subtraction sign to a plus (+) sign and make the second number positive. On the number line, this subtraction is shown by starting at the first number and moving to the right by the absolute value of the second number. You are taking away something negative from the first number, so the first number becomes less negative and may even become positive.
- Example:

$$-6 - (-8) = -6 + (+8) = -6 + 8 = 2$$

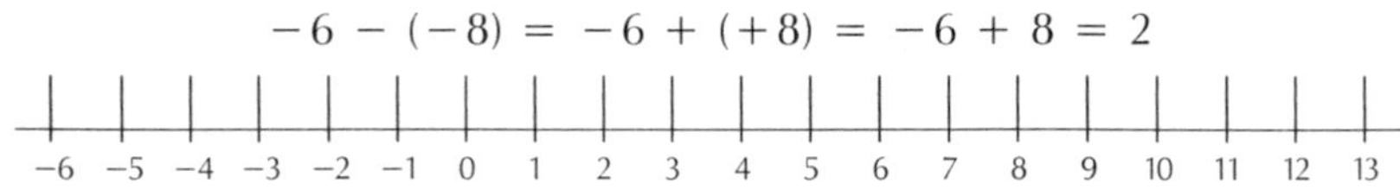

Figure 1.19 Subtracting Negative and Positive Numbers

Adding a Negative Number to a Positive Number

- When you are adding a negative number to a positive number, change the negative sign to a plus (+) sign and the addition sign to a minus (subtraction) sign. On the number line, this addition is shown by starting at the first (positive) number and moving to the left by the absolute value of the second number. You are adding something negative to the first number, so the first number becomes smaller and may even become negative.

- Example:

$$9 + (-12) = 9 - (+12) = 9 - 12 = -3$$

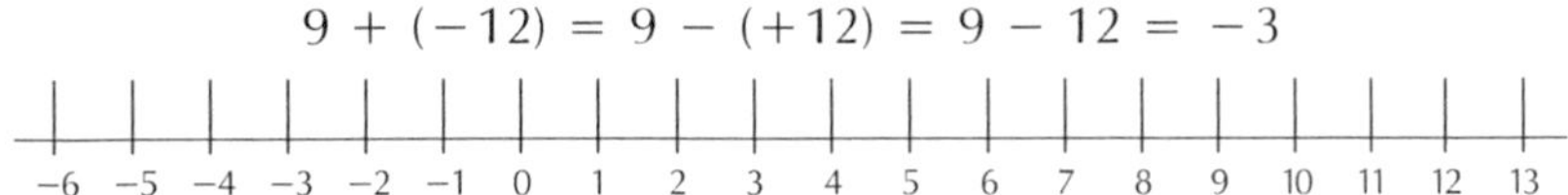

Adding Two Negative Numbers

- When you are adding two negative numbers, the first number is going to become even more negative (smaller). On the number line, this addition is shown by starting at the first negative number and moving to the left by the absolute value of the second number. You are adding something negative to something that is already negative, so the answer is even more negative than either of the two numbers.
- Example:

$$-2 + (-3) = -5$$

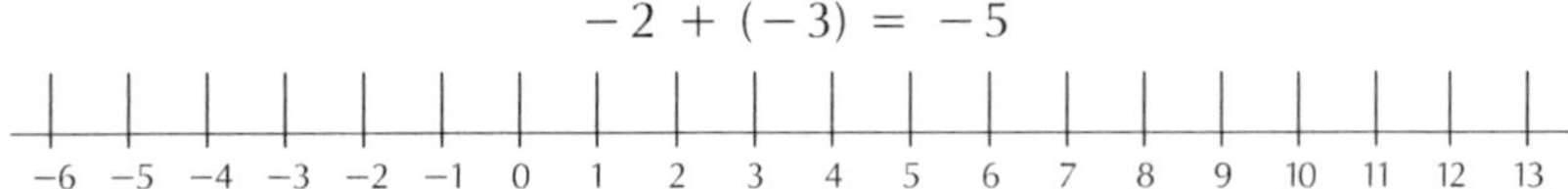

Adding a Positive Number to a Negative Number

- When you are adding a positive number to a negative number, the first number is going to become less negative and may even become positive. On the number line, this addition is shown by starting at the negative number and moving to the right by the value of the second number. You are adding something positive to something that is negative, so the answer is less negative and may even become positive.
- Example:

$$-5 + 10 = 5$$

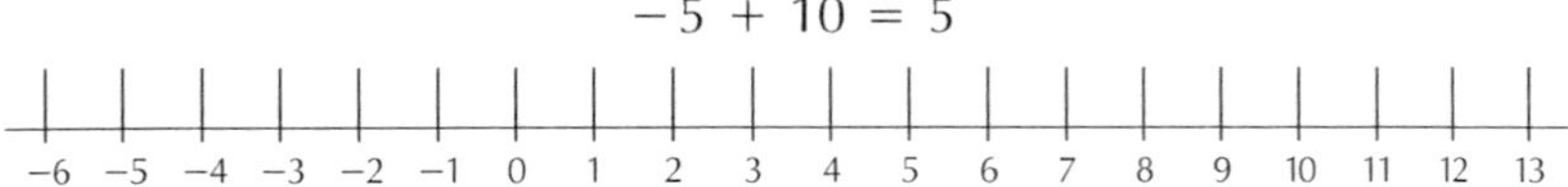

Adding Two Positive Numbers

- When you are adding two positive numbers, the answer is going to be larger than either of the two numbers. On the number line, this addition is shown by starting at the first number and moving to the right by the value of the second number. You are adding something positive to something that is already positive, so the answer must be positive and be larger than either of the two numbers.

- Example:

$$3 + 4 = 7$$

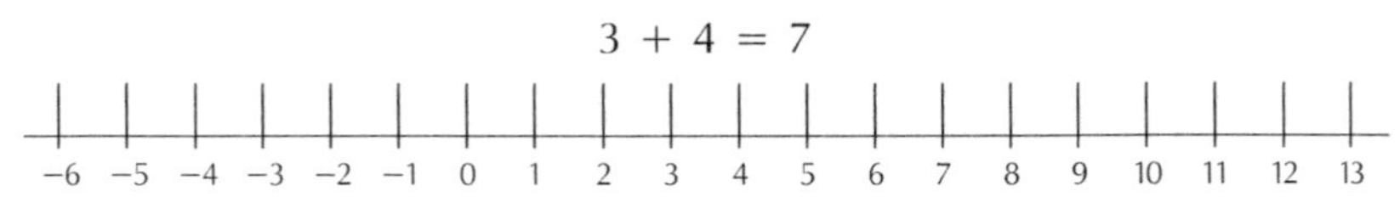

Figure 1.20 Rules for Changing Signs and Moving on the Number Line Adding

1.5 HOMEWORK: CONVERSIONS AND BASIC MATHEMATICAL OPERATIONS CONVERSIONS

Approximate conversions will come naturally to you after you live in the United States for a few years. Here are some exercises for your homework.

Fill in the blank with a correct word or phrase:

1. 5 yards is ______________________ 5 meters.
2. 28 grams is ______________________ 1 ounce.
3. 1 mile is ______________________ 1 kilometer.
4. 5 liters is ______________________ 1 gallon.
5. 500 milliliters (ml) is ______________________ 1 pint.
6. 1 c. is ______________________ 250 ml.
7. 5,000 ft. is ______________________ 1,000 meters.
8. 25°C is ______________________ 75°F.
9. 2 kilograms (kg) is ______________________ 4.5 lbs.
10. 10 square meters is ______________________ 100 square ft. (sf).
11. 1 square yard is ______________________ 1 square meter.
12. 100 kg is ______________________ 200 lbs.
13. 24 oz. is ______________________ 3 c.
14. 2 quarts is ______________________ 2 l.
15. 2 gallons is ______________________ 8 qts.
16. 4 pints is ______________________ 1/2 gal.
17. 1 liter is ______________________ 4 c.
18. 167 cm is ______________________ 66 in.

19. 6′7″ is ____________________ 2 m.
20. 30 cm is ____________________ 1 foot.

Convert from metric to ASM. Use the appropriate qualifier (about, more than, less than, close to, the same as).

21. 4 liters is ____________________.
22. 5 cm is ____________________.
23. 250 ml is ____________________.
24. 3 km is ____________________.
25. 5,000 m is ____________________.
26. 500 g is ____________________.
27. 4 kg is ____________________.
28. 28°C is ____________________.
29. 0°C is ____________________.
30. 1,600 m is ____________________.
31. 400 m is ____________________.
32. 5 ml is ____________________.
33. 15 ml is ____________________.
34. 1,000 ml is ____________________.
35. 1/2 liter is ____________________.
36. 500 km is ____________________.
37. 2,500 m is ____________________.
38. 450 deciliter (dl) is ____________________.
39. 50 ml is ____________________.
40. 1.6 km is ____________________.

Convert from ASM to metric:

41. 1 mi. is ____________________.
42. 212°F is ____________________.
43. 350°F is ____________________.
44. 1 qt. is ____________________.
45. 1 c. is ____________________.
46. 1 pint is ____________________.
47. 1 lb. is ____________________.
48. 5′11″ is ____________________.

49. 1/2 c. is ______________________________.
50. 1 gallon (gal) is ______________________________.
51. 4 oz. is ______________________________.
52. 800 sf is ______________________________.
53. 5 acres is ______________________________.
54. 30 miles per hour (mph) is ______________________________.
55. 1,000 mi. is ______________________________.
56. 2,000′ is ______________________________.
57. 2,000 yds. is ______________________________.
58. 150 lb. is ______________________________.
59. 1/2 mi. is ______________________________.
60. 5 lbs. is ______________________________.
61. 2 tsp is ______________________________.
62. 4 tbs is ______________________________.

Add or subtract the following, showing your answer on the number line.

63. $4 + 7 =$

64. $4 - 7 =$

65. $4 + (-7) =$

−6 −5 −4 −3 −2 −1 0 1 2 3 4 5 6 7 8 9 10 11 12 13

66. $4 - (-7) =$

−6 −5 −4 −3 −2 −1 0 1 2 3 4 5 6 7 8 9 10 11 12 13

67. $-5 + 12 =$

−6 −5 −4 −3 −2 −1 0 1 2 3 4 5 6 7 8 9 10 11 12 13

68. $-2 + (-4) =$

69. $-6 - (-7) =$

−6 −5 −4 −3 −2 −1 0 1 2 3 4 5 6 7 8 9 10 11 12 13

70. $-3 - 3 =$

−6 −5 −4 −3 −2 −1 0 1 2 3 4 5 6 7 8 9 10 11 12 13

Solve the following equations, keeping in mind the rules for Order of Operations:

71. $5 + (7 - 3)(5 - 6) =$
72. $b(c + a) + bc + ba =$
73. $(14)(6 \div 2) + 4 - (-9) =$
74. $(15 \cdot 4)(4 \div 2) - 7 + (-9) - 18 =$

Solve the following word problem:

75. Joselyn is going to drive from her college to a friend's house. Her college is in Boulder, Colorado, and her friend lives in Las Vegas, Nevada. Another friend told Joselyn that it takes 13 hours to drive 1,300 km to Las Vegas. Joselyn knows her car has a 50-liter fuel (gas) tank and gets 12 km per liter of fuel.

Joselyn tends to get hungry and thirsty when she drives, so she needs to go shopping for some food and drinks. She expects she will need 250 grams of sliced turkey and 100 grams of sliced cheese for her trip, and three liters of water. She also likes chocolate, so she plans to buy 300 grams.

Of course, since she's in America, Joselyn needs you to help her convert the metric measurements to ASM measurements.

Use your ASM and metric conversion skills to answer the following questions:

a. How many miles will Joselyn be driving to get from Boulder to Las Vegas?

b. How many miles per hour (mph) does she expect to drive as her average speed?
c. How many gallons of gas does Joselyn's car's fuel tank hold?
d. How many miles per gallon of fuel does her car get?
e. Will Joselyn need to refill (refuel) her car during her trip?
f. How many times will she need to refuel?
g. How many gallons of gasoline will Joselyn need for her trip to Las Vegas?
h. How many ounces of turkey does she need to buy? How many pounds is that?
i. How many ounces of cheese will Joselyn need to buy?
j. How many pounds of chocolate does she need? How many ounces is that?

(The correct answers follow chapter 6.)

2

Estimating, Approximating, and Rounding

Rounding and estimating are two ways to make numbers easier (simpler) to manage (work with). Many numbers are too large or have decimals (such as dollars and cents), and they are easier to add, subtract, multiply, and divide if you "round them off" first. The answer you get will be close to the true (real) answer, but it won't be exact (precise). The same applies when you estimate something: The answer will be close, but not exact.

2.1 ROUNDING

When you "round" a number, you are making it either a bit (slightly) larger or slightly (a bit) smaller. There are rules for doing this. These rules ensure that your answer is close enough to be useful. Take a look at sidebar 2.1 to get a basic idea of the value (use) of rounding.

Why would you want to round numbers? To make them easier to use (work with). Even if you have a calculator, it takes time to enter large numbers and decimals. Each extra number (digit) you enter into a calcula-

> **Rounding**
>
> Think of "rounding" as taking something with sharp edges and making it smoother (less sharp, less precise). When you file something (such as wood or your nails), you are rounding it. You still have almost the same thing as before, but the edges are smoother and easier to work with.

Sidebar 2.1

tor makes it more likely you might make a mistake (error). Each extra number you have to consider when adding, subtracting, multiplying, or dividing makes it more likely that you might make an error (mistake). When you are trying to estimate your total at the grocery store, rounding each price makes the process of estimating easier. Figure 2.1 shows you some of the advantages of rounding.

How do you know when to round a number up to the next highest number, and when to round it down? Take a look at the next chart (figure 2.2).

For decimals, the chart is similar (see figure 2.3).

Note that the two charts look almost the same. However, you should not round both the decimal part of a number and the whole-number part. If a number has both a decimal part and a whole-number part, you normally only round the decimal part.

2.1.1 Rounding to the Nearest Whole Number

The first example in this section involves rounding to the nearest whole number. When you round a decimal so there is no longer a decimal com-

- If Vladimir is buying items that cost \$4.56, \$12.98, \$3.22, \$8.33, \$0.78, \$0.43, \$2.12, \$13.76, \$5.67, \$34.32, and \$0.50, it is much easier to round the numbers to get rid of (eliminate) the cents (¢) portion. But you don't want to change the prices too much or your estimate (answer) won't be very accurate. When you apply the rules of rounding below, you can estimate the price of each item like this:

  \$4.56 is \$5.00
  \$12.98 is \$13.00
  \$3.22 is \$3.00
  \$0.78 is \$1.00
  \$0.43 is \$0
  \$2.12 is \$2.00
  \$13.76 is \$14.00
  \$5.67 is \$6.00
  \$34.32 is \$34.00
  \$0.50 is \$1.00

- This is called rounding to the nearest whole number.

Figure 2.1 Rounding and Estimating at the Store

When a Whole Number Ends In:	Terminology	Do This:
0, 1, 2, 3, 4	Rounding to the nearest 10	Round down
5, 6, 7, 8, 9	Rounding to the nearest 10	Round up
0 through 49	Rounding to the nearest 100	Round down
50 through 99	Rounding to the nearest 100	Round up
0 through 499	Rounding to the nearest 1,000	Round down
500 through 999	Rounding to the nearest 1,000	Round up
0 through 4,999	Rounding to the nearest 10,000	Round down
5,000 through 9,999	Rounding to the nearest 10,000	Round up
0 through 49,999	Rounding to the nearest 100,000	Round down
50,000 through 99,000	Rounding to the nearest 100,000	Round up
0 through 499,999	Rounding to the nearest 1,000,000	Round down
500,000 through 999,000	Rounding to the nearest 1,000,000	Round up

Figure 2.2 Whole Number Rounding Chart

ponent (part), you are rounding to the nearest whole number. Figure 2.4 explains the process of rounding decimals up to get a whole number.

If you want to round the whole-number part of a number that contains a decimal, you must get rid of (eliminate) the decimal part first. You cannot round the decimal part to 1 or 0 and then round the resulting whole number. That is "double rounding" and will result in answers (results) that are not very accurate. Figure 2.5 shows what would happen if you tried to "double round" a number.

What does the information in the double-rounding chart mean? First, you have to decide how much to round a number. In the example at the

When a Decimal Ends In:	Terminology	Do This:
0, 1, 2, 3, 4	Rounding to the nearest tenth	Round down
5, 6, 7, 8, 9	Rounding to the nearest tenth	Round up
0 through 49	Rounding to the nearest hundredth	Round down
50 through 99	Rounding to the nearest hundredth	Round up
0 through 499	Rounding to the nearest thousandth	Round down
500 through 999	Rounding to the nearest thousandth	Round up
0 through 4,999	Rounding to the nearest ten thousandth	Round down
5,000 through 9,999	Rounding to the nearest ten thousandth	Round up
0 through 49,999	Rounding to the nearest hundred thousandth	Round down
50,000 through 99,000	Rounding to the nearest hundred thousandth	Round up
0 through 499,999	Rounding to the nearest millionth	Round down
500,000 through 999,000	Rounding to the nearest millionth	Round up

Figure 2.3 Decimal Number Rounding Chart

- If the decimal is 0, 1, 2, 3, or 4 (tenths), round down (the decimal part becomes 0).
- If the decimal is 5, 6, 7, 8, or 9 (tenths), round up (the decimal part becomes 1).
- If the decimal is 00 to 49 (hundredths), round down to 0.
- If the decimal is 50 to 99 (hundredths), round up to 1.
- If the decimal part is 000 to 499 (thousandths), round down to 0.
- If the decimal part is 500 to 999 (thousandths), round up to 1.
- If the decimal part is 0000 to 4999 (ten thousandths), round down to 0.
- If the decimal part is 5000 to 9999 (ten thousandths), round up to 1.
- If the decimal part is 00000 to 49999 (hundred thousandths), round down to 0.
- If the decimal part is 50000 to 99999 (hundred thousandths), round up to 1.
- If the decimal part is 000000 to 499999 (millionths), round down to 0.
- If the decimal part is 500000 to 999999 (millionths), round up to 1.

Figure 2.4 Rounding Decimals to Whole Numbers

beginning of this section, Vladimir decided to round to the nearest dollar (a whole number), so he used the 00 through 49 and 50 through 99 rule on the decimal-rounding chart. Numbers between $0.00 and $0.49 are rounded to zero (0). Numbers between $0.50 and $0.99 are rounded to $1.00. If he had decided to round to the nearest tenth, he would have looked at the last number of each price and rounded numbers between 0 and 4 down to 0 and numbers between 5 and 9 up to 10. As mentioned earlier, when you round a number, there are rules to follow. The rules for Vladimir's situation are shown in figure 2.6.

2.1.2 Practice Exercises

Rounding Whole Numbers

Round the following numbers (refer to the Whole-Number Rounding Chart and the examples in section 2.1).

a. Round 457 to the nearest 10 ________________
b. Round 13,099 to the nearest 1,000 ________________
c. Round 456 to the nearest 100 ________________

- If you want to round the whole-number portion of 37.765, you must first drop (get rid of, eliminate) the decimal portion. Now you have 37, and you can round the whole number.
- If you want to round 37.765 to the nearest whole number, you would round up since the decimal part (component) is between 500 and 999. The result (answer) would be 38.
- Why do you think you only round a number once?
- Double rounding may make your final answer too large. Look at the next number and see what happens if you round the decimal part and then the whole number part, and then look at what happens if you drop the decimal part and then round the whole number part.

    Example: Double rounding (rounding the decimal and then rounding the whole number)

    - Round 49.87.
    - The decimal part becomes 1.0, so the value is now 50.
    - Rounding 50, you get 100 (round up) if you are rounding to the nearest 100 or 50 if you are rounding to the nearest 10.

    Example: Single rounding (dropping the decimal and then rounding the whole number)

    - Round 49.87.
    - Drop the decimal part so you have 49.
    - Rounding 49, you get 0 if you are rounding to the nearest 100 or 50 if you are rounding to the nearest 10.
- A bit of a difference if you're rounding to the nearest 100!

Figure 2.5 Double Rounding

d. Round 456 to the nearest 10 ______________
e. Round 100,009 to the nearest 1,000 ______________
f. Round 100,009 to the nearest 10 ______________

Answers:

a. 460 (round up since the 0 to 9 digit is between 5 and 9)
b. 13,000 (round down since the 100s digits are between 000 and 499)
c. 500 (round up since the 10s digits are between 50 and 99)
d. 460 (round up since the 0 to 9 digit is between 5 and 9)
e. 100,000 (round down since the 100s digits are between 000 and 499)
f. 100,010 (round up since the 0 to 9 digit is between 5 and 9)

- Rounding to the nearest dollar, $2.49 becomes $2.00—you round down since the decimal portion is between 0¢ and 49¢. If you round $2.49 to the nearest tenth, you look at the last digit (number) and round it up since it is between 5 and 9. In this case, rounding $2.49 is $2.5. Since we write prices with two decimal places, the actual answer is $2.50. Writing $2.5 is not wrong, but it is not really right (correct) either.
- Rounding to the nearest dollar, $2.50 becomes $3.00—you round up since the decimal portion is between 50¢ and 99¢. If you round $2.50 to the nearest tenth, you look at the last number and round it down since it is between 0 and 4. In this case, rounding $2.50 is $2.5. Since we write prices with two decimal places, the actual answer is $2.50. Writing $2.5 is not wrong, but it is not really right (correct) either.
- Rounding to the nearest dollar, $2.55 becomes $3.00—you round up since the decimal portion is between 50¢ and 99¢. If you round $2.55 to the nearest tenth, you look at the last number and round up since it is between 5 and 9. In this case, rounding $2.55 is $2.6. Since we write prices with two decimal places, the actual answer is $2.60. Writing $2.6 is not wrong, but it is not really right (correct) either.
- Note: If you were rounding any other type of decimal (other than money), you would not need to add the zero.

Figure 2.6 Rounding Rules

Rounding Numbers That Include a Decimal Component

Round the following numbers (refer to the Decimal Rounding Chart and the examples in section 2.1).

a. Round 45.67 to the nearest tenth ________________
b. Round 0.67 to the nearest tenth ________________
c. Round 1,002.45 to the nearest whole number ________________
d. Round 99.77 to the nearest whole number ________________
e. Round 34.9987 to the nearest thousandth ________________
f. Round 0.987 to the nearest hundredth ________________

Answers:

a. 45.7 (round up since the hundredths digit is between 5 and 9)
b. 0.7 (round up since the hundredths digit is between 5 and 9)

c. 1,002 (round the decimal part to 0 since the decimal is between 00 and 49)
d. 100 (round the decimal part to 1 since the decimal part is between 50 and 99; you must then add the 1 to the whole-number part)
e. 34.999 (round up since the last two digits are between 50 and 99)
f. 0.99 (round up since the thousandths digit is between 5 and 9)

2.2 ESTIMATING AND APPROXIMATING

When you apply the principles of rounding, you do so to estimate or approximate something.

For example:

When you need to buy new carpet, first you measure the room. Then you calculate the square yards or square feet of carpet you need. If the number is not an easy one to remember, you round it up to an easier number. This number is an estimation or approximation. It is close enough to allow you to shop for carpet. If you tell the salesperson "I need about 100 square yards of carpet," you can get a good idea of the cost. Maybe you really need 97.3 square yards. By asking the price of 100 square yards, you won't be surprised later when you have to pay for 97.3 square yards, and 100 is easier to remember (work with) than 97.3.

When you buy something where the exact amount is not important, an estimate or approximation may be all you need. If you are looking for an apartment or house, and you need about 800 square feet, you probably don't care if the size (that is, the floor space) is 790 or 810 square feet. If the landlord says the apartment is approximately 800 square feet, you aren't going to care if it is actually 787 square feet. You may care if it is actually only 710 square feet, though! If you round 787 to the nearest hundred, you get 800. If you round 710 to the nearest hundred, you only get 700. That is a big (significant) difference!

How do you apply (use) estimating in the real world? Let's look at figure 2.7—an example for buying carpet (floor coverings).

2.3 APPROXIMATING, ESTIMATING, AND ROUNDING IN THE REAL WORLD

As we mentioned earlier, there are times when you need to break the rules for estimating, rounding, and approximating. Before you can break (not

- You are planning to buy new carpet for your house. You have measured the living room, and it is 20.3 feet by 14.6 feet. For ease (simplicity) of calculating (figuring out) approximately how much carpet you need, you can round 20.3 feet down to 20 feet and 14.6 feet up to 15 feet. Carpet is normally sold and priced in square yards (which are similar to square meters). You might even round 20.3 feet *up* to 21 feet to be sure you didn't underestimate the amount of carpet you will need. You need to do several calculations before you go shopping.
- First, figure out the square footage, which is the area the carpet must cover. To do that, multiply 20 feet by (times) 15 feet. You should get 300 square feet (sf). You probably can do this in your head or on a piece of paper.
- Note that if you did the exact calculation, you might need a calculator to avoid a mistake. The exact measurement is 296.38 sf, which is very close to the estimated answer of 300 sf.
- Since carpet is usually sold by the square yard, you need to refer to the tables that give you the foot → yard conversion. There are 3 feet in each yard. Since you multiply 2 measurements in feet together to get the area, you need to divide your answer by 9 (3 × 3) to get the square yards. You can also divide each measurement (15 feet and 20 feet) by 3, but then you have numbers that are harder to work with.
- Dividing 300 by 9 gives you 33.33 square yards. Since you are only shopping for prices, you probably should not round this number down. This is a case where it is better to round *up* to 34 or even 35 square yards to avoid surprises (mistakes) later!
- Now you have the information you need to go shopping. It is a good idea to have both the square feet (300) and square yard (about 34 square yards) measurements when you get to the carpet store.

Figure 2.7 Buying Carpet

follow) a rule, though, you must understand the reason for the rule. The first two sections of this chapter explained the rules and showed you what could happen if you broke the rules. Now that you have seen some of the potential problems, let's look at times when you apply some of the rules you just learned but can break some of them, too.

Here are some situations (examples) when you should not precisely (completely) follow the rules of estimating, approximating, and rounding.

1. Buying carpet, tile, linoleum, hardwood, or other flooring materials (floor coverings). It is almost always better to round each measurement to

the next higher (greater) whole number. This will make the price you are given closer to the final price.
2. If you are trying to lose weight, a "trick" is to round up the number of calories in an item (meal, fruit, piece of bread, etc.) so you will think you ate more than you really did.
3. If you are trying to lose weight by exercising, it is better to round down the number of calories you think you used (walking, running, biking, housecleaning, or at the gym). This way, you will think you need to work a bit harder, and then you might lose weight faster (more quickly).
4. When you go to the grocery store, it is easy to round all prices up to the nearest dollar. This makes keeping an approximate total easy, and you won't try to spend too much money, either.
5. When you are loading a vehicle or trailer, it is better to round the weight of each item up to the nearest pound, rather than round it down. This will make it less likely you overload (put too much in) the trailer or vehicle.

Any time in which it is better to *over*estimate, you should round all the numbers up. Any time it is better to *under*estimate, it is better to round all the numbers down.

2.4 HOMEWORK: ROUNDING, ESTIMATING, AND APPROXIMATING

2.4.1 Rounding Whole Numbers

Round the following whole numbers up or down, using the rules for rounding whole numbers.

1. 47 (to the nearest ten)________________
2. 5,670 (to the nearest hundred)________________
3. 47 (to the nearest hundred)________________
4. 51 (to the nearest hundred)________________
5. 876 (to the nearest ten)________________
6. 14,567 (to the nearest thousand)________________
7. 345,234 (to the nearest hundred)________________
8. 345,234 (to the nearest thousand)________________
9. 345,234 (to the nearest ten thousand)________________

10. 345,234 (to the nearest hundred thousand)______________
11. 5 (to the nearest ten)______________
12. 1,090 (to the nearest ten)______________
13. 1,090 (to the nearest hundred)______________
14. 961 (to the nearest ten)______________
15. 961 (to the nearest hundred)______________
16. 4,549 (to the nearest ten)______________
17. 4,549 (to the nearest hundred)______________
18. 4,549 (to the nearest thousand)______________
19. 3,432,456 (to the nearest hundred thousand)______________
20. 3,432,456 (to the nearest hundred)______________

2.4.2 Rounding Numbers with a Decimal Component

Round the following with decimal components up or down, using the rules for rounding decimals.

21. 0.034 (round to the nearest hundredth)______________
22. 3.45 (round to the nearest tenth)______________
23. 0.7089 (round to the nearest hundredth)______________
24. 45.988 (round to the nearest tenth) ______________
25. 100.991 (round to the nearest hundredth)______________
26. 100.991 (round to the nearest tenth)______________
27. 0.7446 (round to the nearest thousandth)______________
28. 0.7446 (round to the nearest hundredth)______________
29. 509.667 (round to the nearest whole number)______________
30. 509.667 (round to the nearest hundredth)______________
31. 0.00015 (round to the nearest ten thousandth)______________
32. 0.00015 (round to the nearest thousandth)______________
33. 0.51 (round to the nearest tenth)______________
34. 4.098743 (round to the nearest whole number)______________
35. 4.098743 (round to the nearest tenth)______________
36. 4.098743 (round to the nearest thousandth)______________
37. 4.098743 (round to the nearest ten thousandth)______________
38. 0.60643 (round to the nearest hundredth)______________
39. 0.60643 (round to the nearest thousandth)______________
40. 0.60643 (round to the nearest tenth)______________

2.4.3 Estimating and Approximating

Use the rules for rounding decimals and whole numbers, and then estimate or approximate the answer. Avoid double rounding!

41. You need to buy carpet for a room that measures 30.4′ by 14.5′. If you round to the nearest whole number, how many square feet of carpet do you need to buy? ____________
42. Convert the answer in question 41 to square yards. About how many square yards of carpet do you need to buy? Is your answer reasonable? ____________
43. You need to buy 4.6 yards of fabric to make a dress. You need another 2.4 yards of the same fabric to make a costume for your daughter for her school's graduation dance. How many yards should you buy to make sure you have enough material? ____________
44. It usually takes you 2 hours to do your English homework and 4.5 hours to finish your math homework. It is now noon (12:00). You plan to go to a concert tonight, and it takes about 1 hour to drive there, and ½ hour to find parking. The concert starts at 7 p.m. Do you have enough time to get everything done and arrive at the concert on time? How much time do you think you should allow (budget, plan) to do everything? Remember that everything takes longer than you expect! ____________
45. You plan to paint your living room. It is rectangular. The long dimension (length) is 22.5 feet. The short dimension (width) is 10.7 feet. The room is 8′ high. How many square feet of wall do you have to paint? (Remember that there are two of each wall.) ____________
46. 1 gallon of paint covers 350 square feet of wall. How many gallons of paint do you estimate you will need for this job? ____________
47. If 1 gallon of paint covered 575 square feet of wall, would you be comfortable buying just one can? Why or why not? ____________
48. You are going to drive across the Mojave Desert. It is 400 miles between service stations. You just filled your car's fuel tank about 100 miles earlier, before entering the desert. Your tank holds 15 gallons of fuel, and you get (can travel) about 33 miles per gallon of gasoline. You are right next to (in front of) the last gas (service) station for 400 miles.

a. How many gallons of fuel did you use already? ____________
b. How many gallons do you have left? ____________

c. How many miles can you drive with that amount of fuel (assuming you average 33 miles per gallon)? ______________
d. Should you fill the car's gas tank now, or take your chances? ______________

49. If the person driving across the Mojave Desert didn't approximate the amount of fuel the trip would take, what might happen? ____________
50. It is 120°F in the shade in the Mojave Desert. About how hot is that in centigrade? ____________

2.4.4 Breaking the Rounding, Estimating, and Approximating Rules

Sometimes you should round up even if the rules say otherwise. Sometimes you should round down even if the rules indicate not to do so. Think about the result you need or want when answering these questions.

51. You have measured your room for carpet and think you need 52 square yards. However, you weren't sure how to measure around the closet and fireplace. Should you get prices for 50 or 55 square yards? Why? ____

52. You are trying to lose weight. All the diet meals in your freezer are 365 calories. You want to try to "fool" yourself and eat fewer calories. How should you round the calories in the meal—to the nearest ten or the nearest hundred? ____________
53. The same meals have 349 calories.

a. If you round to the nearest ten, you get _________.
b. If you round to the nearest hundred, you get _________.
c. If you break the rules and round up to the nearest hundred, what do you get? _________

2.4.5 Real-World Word Problems

54. You are looking for an apartment. You want to be sure your furniture will fit between the windows, so you have measured the width of your

table, bed, and sofa. The table is 64 inches, the bed is 79 inches, and the sofa is 93 inches. The landlord has told you the space between the windows in the kitchen (for the table) is 70 inches, the space for the bed is 80 inches, and the space for the sofa is 90 inches. She told you she rounded the numbers using the rules for rounding to the nearest ten.

a. If you round your furniture's measurements, what do you get?
   Table ________ Bed________ Sofa________
b. What is the range of possible values for the apartment measurements since they have been rounded?
   Kitchen window space ____________
   Bedroom window space ____________
   Living room window space ____________
c. Which measurements should concern you? Where will your furniture fit, and where is the space (fit) uncertain (questionable)?
d. What area(s) do you need to ask the landlord to remeasure? (Hint: You will need to know the exact amount of space for at least one of your pieces of furniture. The rounded amount seems too small, but may not be.)

55. Matthew is planning to buy a new suit for a job interview. His friend told him he needed to measure around his neck, chest, and waist, and also measure the length of his leg and arm. Michael measures himself and gets the following results:

Neck:	16.5″
Chest:	43″
Waist:	35″
Arm length:	32.5″
Leg length:	34″

Matthew has never bought clothes in America before, so he decides to round each measurement to the nearest ten (for his chest, waist, and leg measurements) and to the nearest whole number (for his arm and neck measurements).

When Matthew gets to the store, he finds out that chest measurements need to be rounded to the nearest even number, waist measurements to the nearest whole number, neck measurements to the nearest 1/2-inch, arm lengths to the nearest whole number, and leg measurements to the nearest whole number.

a. What are Matthew's estimated measurements?
   Neck ________
   Waist ________
   Chest ________
   Arm length ________
   Leg length ________
b. What should the rounded measurements be?
   Neck ________
   Waist ________
   Chest ________
   Arm length ________
   Leg length ________
c. Do you think it is a good idea to round clothing measurements to the nearest ten? Why or why not?

(The correct answers follow chapter 6.)

3

Writing Numbers in Words and Words in Numbers

In this chapter you will learn how to write fractions, decimals, whole numbers, hybrid numbers, percents, and other types of numbers in words, and convert numbers written as words back to actual numbers. You will learn when to place a hyphen between words and when to write numbers in words. Being able to properly write numbers in words and convert (change) from words to numbers is very important when writing checks and paying bills. In the last section of this chapter, I've included some examples to show why you sometimes need to ignore some of the rounding and estimating rules, too.

3.1 WRITING ACTUAL NUMBERS IN WORDS

In this section we will look at both whole numbers and decimals. Whole numbers do not have a decimal component (part). Decimals may or may not have a whole number part (element component).

3.1.1 Whole Numbers

First, let's look at how you write whole numbers using (in) words. Whole numbers are numbers that do not include fractions or decimals. It may help you to think of whole numbers as dollars, and fractions or decimals as cents. There are other considerations, too—especially concerning the use of hyphens. Figure 3.1 explains the Rule of Hyphens.

In American English, certain numbers are always connected with a hyphen. Take a look at the chart below. Note that all numbers in words, from

- Most numbers between 21 and 99 are hyphenated.
- The exceptions are 30, 40, 50, 60, 70, 80, and 90.

Figure 3.1 The Rule of Hyphens

21 through 99, are hyphenated, except 20, 30, 40, 50, 60, 70, 80, and 90. This rule of hyphens applies to whole numbers, decimals, and fractions. Look at the *Number/Word Conversion Table* (table 3.1) for a complete display (listing) of the numbers from one 1 to 100.

Numbers above 99 are "hybrid" numbers because they have two parts. When you write actual numbers in words, you need to think in sets (groups) of three. For whole numbers, the last two digits (numbers)—the ones to the right—in each set of three will be between 1 and 99. Keep in mind the rules for hyphenation. If the two right-hand numbers in each set of three are between 21 and 99, you need to apply the Rule of Hyphens. For whole numbers, when counting by threes, always start at the far right. (If there are decimals involved, the rule is similar, but not the same.) There is always a comma (not a period) to the left of each third number, too. Look at the Number Value Chart in figure 3.2.

Note the *italicized columns* in figure 3.2. They are special because they contain the numbers that are hyphenated. Look at the parts in *italics*. The numbers 10–99 are highlighted in *italics*. Remember that *most* numbers between 21 and 99 are hyphenated. The numbers in *italics* fall between 10 and 99. That means that *most* numbers that fall in the columns for *tens*, *ten thousands*, *ten millions*, *ten billions*, and so forth are hyphenated when they are between 21 and 99 . Remember that numbers between 1 and 19, as well as 20, 30, 40, 50, 60, 70, 80, and 90, are never hyphenated. Refer to the Number/Word Chart (table 3.1) in section 3.1 to refresh your memory.

We are only looking at whole numbers in the first part of this chapter. When you write whole numbers in words, you do not use "and" to connect the words. When we write decimals and fractions in words, we *do* use "and." Figure 3.3 is the Rule of "and" for Whole Numbers.

For Example:

- 1,021 is written as one thousand twenty-one. Note that only the "twenty-one" is hyphenated. The 21 is in the "tens" column in figure

Table 3.1 Word/Number Conversions

One	1	Thirty-five	35	Sixty-nine	69
Two	2	Thirty-six	36	Seventy	70
Three	3	Thirty-seven	37	Seventy-one	71
Four	4	Thirty-eight	38	Seventy-two	72
Five	5	Thirty-nine	39	Seventy-three	73
Six	6	Forty	40	Seventy-four	74
Seven	7	Forty-one	41	Seventy-five	75
Eight	8	Forty-two	42	Seventy-six	76
Nine	9	Forty-three	43	Seventy-seven	77
Ten	10	Forty-four	44	Seventy-eight	78
Eleven	11	Forty-five	45	Seventy-nine	79
Twelve	12	Forty-six	46	Eighty	80
Thirteen	13	Forty-seven	47	Eighty-one	81
Fourteen	14	Forty-eight	48	Eighty-two	82
Fifteen	15	Forty-nine	49	Eighty-three	83
Sixteen	16	Fifty	50	Eighty-four	84
Seventeen	17	Fifty-one	51	Eighty-five	85
Eighteen	18	Fifty-two	52	Eighty-six	86
Nineteen	19	Fifty-three	53	Eighty-seven	87
Twenty	20	Fifty-four	54	Eighty-eight	88
Twenty-one	21	Fifty-five	55	Eighty-nine	89
Twenty-two	22	Fifty-six	56	Ninety	90
Twenty-three	23	Fifty-seven	57	Ninety-one	91
Twenty-four	24	Fifty-eight	58	Ninety-two	92
Twenty-five	25	Fifty-nine	59	Ninety-three	93
Twenty-six	26	Sixty	60	Ninety-four	94
Twenty-seven	27	Sixty-one	61	Ninety-five	95
Twenty-eight	28	Sixty-two	62	Ninety-six	96
Twenty-nine	29	Sixty-three	63	Ninety-seven	97
Thirty	30	Sixty-four	64	Ninety-eight	98
Thirty-one	31	Sixty-five	65	Ninety-nine	99
Thirty-two	32	Sixty-six	66	One hundred	100
Thirty-three	33	Sixty-seven	67		
Thirty-four	34	Sixty-eight	68		

Ten Millions	*10*,000,000 to *99*,999,999
Millions	1,000,000 to 9,999,999
Hundred Thousands	100,000 to 999,999
Ten Thousands	*10*,000 to *99*,000
Thousands	1,000 to 9,999
Hundreds	100 to 999
Tens	*10* to *99*
Ones	0 to 9

Figure 3.2 Number Values

Whole numbers are not connected using "and."

Figure 3.3 The Rule of "and" for Whole Numbers

3.2. (Note also that we do not write [or say] one thousand *and* twenty-one.)

- 4,222 is written as four thousand two hundred twenty-two. Note that only the "twenty-two" is hyphenated. The 22 is in the "tens" column in figure 3.2. (We do not write [or say] four thousand two hundred *and* twenty-two.)
- 10,380 is written as ten thousand three hundred eighty. There is no hyphen because there is no hyphen in eighty. Again, we do not use "*and.*"
- 974,334 is written as nine hundred seventy-four thousand three hundred thirty-four. Note that there are *two* hyphenated numbers. There is a 76 in the "ten thousands" column in figure 3.2. The 34 is in the "tens" column in the chart.

3.1.2 Practice Exercises

Writing Actual Numbers in Words

Write the following numbers in words. Be careful to put any hyphens in the correct place. Not all the numbers will have a need for hyphens. Do not use "and" to connect the numbers. Practice saying each number. Look at the Number Values Chart (figure 3.2) if you are not sure when to use hyphens.

a. 88 ________________________________
b. 170 ________________________________
c. 2,089 ________________________________
d. 5,111 ________________________________
e. 5,121 ________________________________
f. 11,435 ________________________________
g. 123,456 ________________________________
h. 986,333 ________________________________

Answers:

a. Eighty-eight (Note the hyphen.)
b. One hundred seventy (No hyphens.)
c. Two thousand eighty-nine (Note the hyphen.)
d. Five thousand one hundred eleven (No hyphens.)
e. Five thousand one hundred twenty-one (Note the hyphen. Don't confuse this example with the example in "d.")
f. Eleven thousand four hundred thirty-five (Note the hyphen.)
g. One hundred twenty-three thousand four hundred fifty-six (Note there are two hyphens since there are two numbers between 21 and 99.)
h. Nine hundred eighty-six thousand three hundred thirty-three (Note there are two hyphens again. There are two numbers between 21 and 99.)

Many business transactions (such as paying bills, buying a money order, writing a check) require you to write the number in both words and numbers. This means you have to convert words to numbers. Hyphens are only used when writing numbers as words, so you must take them out when you write actual numbers. Business involves both dollars (which are whole numbers) and cents (which are written as fractions or decimals). You need to know how to write dollars, cents, and dollars combined with cents.

For example:

- Eleven thousand one hundred ninety-seven is written 11,197.
- Four hundred seventy-five thousand three hundred twenty-two is written as 475,322.
- Ninety-nine is written as 99.
- Five hundred twenty is written as 520.

Changing Whole Numbers Written in Words to Actual Numbers

Write the following words as numbers. Remember that there are no hyphens when you write actual numbers.

a. Forty-four ____________
b. Eighteen ____________
c. Two hundred fifty-three ____________
d. Seven thousand eight hundred ____________
e. Seven thousand eight hundred twenty-six ____________
f. Fifteen thousand four hundred sixty-six ____________
g. One hundred sixty-two thousand seventeen ____________
h. Five hundred seventy-one thousand forty-seven ____________

Answers:

a. 44
b. 18
c. 253
d. 7,800
e. 7,826
f. 15,466
g. 162,017 (Not 162170: There is no number in the "hundreds" space, so you need to put a zero [0] there as a placeholder.)
h. 571,047 (Not 571,470: There is no number in the "hundreds" space, so you need to put a zero [0] there as a placeholder.)

3.1.3 Decimals and Fractions

You use decimals and fractions every day. You use them when you write a check or buy a money order. You use them when you follow (read, make) a recipe. You use them when you count your coins when you receive change. Decimals and fractions are connected to whole numbers using "and."

For example:

The fraction for half of something is written 1/2, and it is spoken or written as "one half." If you have 5 of something and another half of the same thing, you say (pronounce) it as 5 1/2 and say (pronounce) or write it as five *and* one half. Figure 3.4 explains the Rule of "and" for Fractions and Decimals.

There are several rules when you are writing fractions and decimals in words instead of numbers. These rules are explained in figure 3.5.

> When you have a whole number combined with a fraction or decimal, the whole number is connected to the fraction or decimal with "and." Within the fraction or decimal, "and" is not used.

Figure 3.4 The Rule of "and" for Fractions and Decimals

For example:

Fractions written in words.

- 1/2 is written as "one half."

Decimals written in words.

- 0.45 is written as "forty-five one hundredths." Note that the fraction (1/100) is needed to explain the value of the "forty-five."

Whole numbers with fractional parts (components) written in words.

- 27 1/2 is written, in words, as "twenty-seven and one half." Another example, 31 21/37, is written, in words, as "thirty-one and twenty-one thirty-sevenths."

> - When you write a fraction as a word, you *must* use a hyphen to connect the two parts.
> - When you write a decimal in words, you *must* use a hyphen to connect the numbers that are between 20 and 99 (except for 20, 30, 40, 50, 60, 70, 80, and 90).
> - When you write a whole number with a fractional part in words, you *must* do several things. You must use a hyphen to connect numbers between 20 and 99 (except 20, 30, 40, 50, 60, 70, 80, and 90), and you *must* use "and" to connect the fraction and the whole number.
> - When you write a whole number with a decimal part in words, you *must* do several things. You *must* use a hyphen to connect numbers between 20 and 99 (except 20, 30, 40, 50, 60, 70, 80, and 90), and you *must* use "and" to connect the decimal and the whole number.

Figure 3.5 The Rules for Writing Fractions and Decimals in Words

Whole numbers with decimal parts (components) written in words.

- 27.5 is a whole number with a decimal part. When you write it in words, it is "twenty-seven and one half" or "twenty-seven and five tenths." Another example, 31.27, is written, in words, as "thirty-one and twenty-seven one hundredths."

When you need to change fractions or decimals written in words back to numbers, you need to follow the rules in figure 3.6.

Fractions consist of two parts—the numerator (top) and denominator (bottom). There are rules to know for writing each part, as shown in figure 3.7. Fractions have two parts—the numerator (top) and denominator (bot-

- When a fraction with a whole number is written in words: Delete (remove) the "and" and replace it with a hyphen when writing the whole number and fraction as a number.
- When a fraction with a whole number is written as a number: Remove the hyphen and replace it with "and" when writing the whole number and fraction in words.
- When a decimal is written in words: Apply the Rule of Hyphenation for numbers between 21 and 99.
- When a decimal is written in numbers: There are no hyphens or commas.

Figure 3.6 The Rules for Changing Fractions and Decimals to Numbers or Words

Numerators

- The numerator (the top part) is written just like whole numbers. This is true when writing the numerator as a number or in words.

Denominators

- The denominator (the bottom part) is written like whole numbers when writing them in numbers.
- When denominators are written as words, you must add the appropriate ending or nonstandard word shown in the denominator chart (see figure 3.8).

Figure 3.7 The Rule for Writing Fractions

tom). The numerator is written just like the whole numbers in section 3.1.1. The denominator is a bit trickier (more difficult). Since the denominator tells (shows) you that the fraction is less than 1, you have to make an important change when you write it in words. You must add a "th" (or other appropriate ending) to the end of the number. So, 1/1,000 becomes one thousand*th*. And 45/100 becomes forty-five one hundred*ths*. Take a look at the denominator chart in figure 3.8. There are several exceptions, too. See the denominator exception chart in figure 3.9.

Figure 3.10 shows you how to write the numerator and denominator or equivalent decimal in words. In this chart, all the denominators

If the last digit in the denominator is a 1, the ending is ''firsts'' when you are writing the fraction in words.

If the last digit in the denominator is a 2, the ending is ''seconds'' when you are writing the fraction in words.

If the last digit in the denominator is a 3, the ending is ''thirds'' when you are writing the fraction in words.

If the last digit in the denominator is a 4, the ending is ''fourths'' when you are writing the fraction in words.

If the last digit in the denominator is a 5, the ending is ''fifths'' when you are writing the fraction in words.

If the last digit in the denominator is a 6, the ending is ''sixths'' when you are writing the fraction in words.

If the last digit in the denominator is a 7, the ending is ''sevenths'' when you are writing the fraction in words.

If the last digit in the denominator is an 8, the ending is ''eighths'' when you are writing the fraction in words.

If the last digit in the denominator is a 9, the ending is ''ninths'' when you are writing the fraction in words.

If the last digit in the denominator is a 10, the ending is ''tenths'' when you are writing the fraction in words.

If the last digit in the denominator is a 0, the ending is ''ths'' when you are writing the fraction in words.

There are several exceptions shown in the Denominator Exception Chart that follows (figure 3.9).

Figure 3.8 Denominator Chart

Exceptions: Nonstandard words

- 1/2—The denominator is always written as "half."
- 1/3—The denominator is always written as "third."
- 1/4—The denominator is written as either "fourth" or "quarter."
- 1/5—The denominator is written as "fifth," not "fiveth."
- 1/8—The denominator is written as "eighth," not "eightth."

Figure 3.9 Denominator Exception Chart

are multiples of 10. Pay close attention to the way the denominator is written.

All decimals can also be written as fractions. When you write a decimal as a fraction, you need to count the number of places (numbers) to the *right* of the decimal point. (Remember that in American English, we use a period (dot) to separate whole numbers and decimals!) If there is one number to the right, the number is written in tenths. If there are two numbers to the right, the number is written in hundredths. If there are three numbers to the right of the decimal point, the number is written in thousandths. The next chart (figure 3.11) shows some decimals and how they are written as fractions and how they are written in words.

Obviously writing fractions or decimals as numbers gets hard (complicated) as the fractions or decimals get smaller. Smaller means there are more numbers in the denominator or more numbers to the *right* of the decimal point. Larger means there are fewer (less) numbers to the *right* of the decimal point or in the denominator. Not all fractions or decimals

1/10 or 0.1	2/10 or 0.2
one ten*th*	two ten*ths*
1/100 or 0.01	21/100 or 0.21
one hundred*th*	twenty-one one hundred*ths*
1/1,000 or 0.001	221/1,000 or 0.221
one thousand*th*	two hundred twenty-one one thousand*ths*
1/10,000 or 0.0001	4,555/10,000 or 0.4555
one ten thousand*th*	four thousand five hundred fifty-five ten thousand*ths*

Figure 3.10 Decimal Equivalents Written in Words

Value	Example: Decimal	Example: Fraction	Example: Words
Tenths	0.9	9/10	Nine tenths
	4.7	4 7/10	Four and seven tenths
Hundredths	0.77	77/100	Seventy-seven one hundredths
	73.94	73 94/100	Seventy-three and ninety-four one hundredths
Thousandths	0.834	834/1,000	Eight hundred thirty-four one thousandths
	5.067	5 67/1,000	Five and sixty-seven one thou-sandths
Ten thousandths	0.0456	456/10,000	Four hundred fifty-six ten thou-sandths
	0.7401	7,401/10,000	Seven thousand four hundred one ten thousandths
	456.9034	456 9,034/10,000	Four hundred fifty-six and nine thousand thirty-four ten thou-sandths
Hundred thousandths	0.56789	56,789/100,000	Fifty-six thousand seven hundred eight-nine one hundred thou-sandths
	45.00897	45 897/100,000	Forty-five and eight hundred ninety-seven one hundred thou-sandths
Millionths	0.897076	897,076/1,000,000	Eight hundred ninety-seven thou-sand seventy-six one millionths
	546.089787	546 89787/1,000,000	Five hundred forty-six and eighty-nine thousand seven hundred eighty-seven one millionths
Ten millionths	0.8976546	8,976,546/10,000,000	Eight million nine hundred seventy-six thousand five hun-dred forty-six ten millionths

Figure 3.11 Writing Decimals as Fractions and Fractions as Decimals

have a whole-number component. Figure 3.12 shows a comparison of fractions and decimals without a whole-number component.

However, if you have a whole number combined with a fraction or decimal, the more numbers in the whole number, the larger the combined number. In other words, the more numbers to the *left* of the decimal point, the larger the number. The fewer the numbers to the *left* of the decimal point, the smaller the number. Figure 3.13 shows a comparison of fractions and decimals with whole-number components.

There are a number of fractions you use often. These fractions are shown in figure 3.14. They are also written in words in the chart. Finally, their approximate decimal values are also in the chart.

0.1111 is smaller than 0.44444
0.99999 is larger than 0.8888
5/234 is larger than 9/4555
76/3333 is smaller than 99/333

Figure 3.12 Comparing Decimal and Fraction Values: No Whole-Number Component

445.999 is larger than 44.999
67.9899999 is smaller than 995.99
44 1/2 is larger than 4 1/4
678 455/1,000 is smaller than 6,945 4,677/10,099

Figure 3.13 Comparing Decimal and Fraction Values: With a Whole-Number Component

Common Fraction	Written in Words	Decimal Equivalent
1/12	one twelfth	0.0833
1/8	one eighth	0.125
1/4	one fourth or one quarter	0.25
1/3	one third	0.333
1/2	one half	0.5
3/4	three fourths or three quarters	0.75

Figure 3.14 Common Fractions and Decimal/Word Equivalents

Knowing where to place commas and decimals is very important. Take a look at sidebar 3.1. Remember that in America, we use commas for whole numbers and periods to separate the decimal component from the whole-number component.

3.1.4 Practice Exercises

Writing Fractions and Decimals in Words: Changing Fractions to Words

Write the following fractions in words. Be careful to put any hyphens in the correct place. Not all the numbers will have a need for hyphens.

> **Commas and Decimals**
>
> There are no commas used to divide (show) sets of three for numbers to the right of the decimal point. Commas are only used to the *left* of the decimal point.

Sidebar 3.1

Use "and" to connect the fractions to the whole numbers. Practice saying each number.

a. 1/2 ________________
b. 1/4 ________________
c. 5 1/2 ________________
d. 21 35/100 ________________
e. 9/12 ________________
f. 115 371/1000 ________________
g. 5/12 ________________
h. 9/16 ________________
i. 24 4/7 ________________
j. 453 5/6 ________________
k. 32 7/8 ________________
l. 4 3/4 ________________

Answers:

a. One half
b. One quarter *or* one fourth
c. Five and one half
d. Twenty-one and thirty-five one hundredths
e. Nine twelfths
f. One hundred fifteen and three hundred seventy-one one thousandths
g. Five twelfths
h. Nine sixteenths
i. Twenty-four and four sevenths
j. Four hundred fifty-three and five sixths

k. Thirty-two and seven eighths
l. Four and three quarters *or* four and three fourths

Changing Decimals to Words

Write the following decimals in words. Be careful to put any hyphens in the correct place. Not all the numbers will have a need for hyphens. Use "and" to connect the fractions to the whole numbers. Practice saying each number.

a. 0.34 ______________________________
b. 44.098 ______________________________
c. 0.333 ______________________________
d. 389.9874 ______________________________
e. 102.091 ______________________________
f. 3.098765 ______________________________
g. 245.78693 ______________________________
h. 0.000001 ______________________________
i. 254.900034 ______________________________
j. 0.5 ______________________________

Answers:

a. Thirty-four one hundredths
b. Forty-four and ninety-eight one thousandths
c. Three hundred thirty-three one thousandths (*or* "about one third")
d. Three hundred eighty-nine and nine thousand eight hundred seventy-four ten thousandths
e. One hundred two and ninety-one one thousandths
f. Three and ninety-eight thousand seven hundred sixty-five one millionths
g. Two hundred forty-five and seventy-eight thousand six hundred ninety-three one hundred thousandths
h. One millionth
i. Two hundred fifty-four and nine hundred thousand thirty-four one millionths
j. One half

Changing Fractions and Decimals Written in Words Back to Numbers: Changing Fractions Written in Words to Numbers

Change the following written fractions to numbers. Practice saying each number.

a. One third ____________________
b. Four and five eighths ____________________
c. Nine thousand and seventeen one thousandths ____________________
d. Six million four hundred twenty-two thousand four hundred ninety-five and seventy-two thousand nine hundred one one hundred thousandths ____________________
e. Two one millionths ____________________
f. Five hundred twenty-two and sixty-seven ten thousandths ____________________
g. One sixteenth ____________________
h. Three and two thirds ____________________
i. Twenty-nine and seventy-three one hundredths ____________________
j. Two quarters *or* two fourths ____________________

Answers:

a. 1/3
b. 4 5/8
c. 9,000.017
d. 6,422,495.72901
e. 0.000002
f. 522.0067
g. 1/16
h. 3 2/3
i. 29.73
j. 2/4 or 1/2

Changing Decimals Written in Words to Numbers

Change the following written decimals to numbers. Practice saying each number.

a. Four one thousandths ______
b. Five and two one hundredths ______
c. Five hundred sixty-seven and nine hundred ninety-nine ten thousandths ______
d. Four hundred and sixty-six one millionths ______
e. Two thousand six hundred one and thirty-three one thousandths ______
f. Nine and seven thousand one ten millionths ______
g. Thirty-three one hundredths ______
h. Five and one half ______
i. Nineteen and four one hundredths ______
j. Two tenths ______

Answers:

a. 0.004
b. 5.02
c. 567.0999
d. 400.000066
e. 2,601.033
f. 9.007001
g. 0.33 or about 1/3
h. 5.5
i. 19.04
j. 0.2

Which Number Is Larger?

a. 999.888 or 99.8888 ______
b. 4,004,002.88 or 44,004,002.8 ______
c. 0.9999 or 0.999 ______
d. 113/1345 or 113/134 ______
e. 6 2/3 or 12 2/33 ______

Answers:

a. 999.888 is larger because there are more digits (numbers) to the left of the decimal point.
b. 44,004,002.8

c. 0.999 because there is not a whole number to the left of the decimal point and there are fewer numbers to the right of the decimal point.
d. 113/134 because there is not a whole number and there are fewer numbers in the denominator.
e. 12 2/33 because there is a whole number and it is larger than the other whole number.

Which Number Is Smaller?

a. 9.99 or 10.999
b. 0.987 or 0.9887

Answers:

a. 9.99
b. 0.987

3.1.5 Percents

You use percents (percentages) every day. Sales tax (VAT, MOM, or GST) is a percent of the total amount of what you purchase. Income tax and other taxes are calculated as a percent of the amount you earn. The amount of interest you earn from your savings account is based on the amount you have saved. Grades in school are written as a percent of correct answers.

In order to multiply or divide something when you have a number written as a percentage, you need to change the percentage to a decimal. Figure 3.15 shows you how to convert percentages to decimals.

For example:

- To convert 26.65% to a decimal, divide by 100. When you divide 26.65 by 100, the answer is 0.2665. Be very careful to put the decimal point in the correct place. Dividing a number by 100 means moving the decimal point two places to the *left*.
- When converting 26% to a decimal, there is no decimal point. But there is an implied decimal point to the right of the last digit (in this

To convert percentages to decimals, divide by 100. To convert decimals to percentages, multiply by 100. If you multiply a number by the percentage without converting it, you must divide the answer by 100.

Figure 3.15 Converting Percentages to Decimal Equivalents

case, the 6). So, when you divide by 100, you must move this implied decimal two places to the *left*. That means 26% becomes 0.26.

- To convert 126.65% to a decimal form, remember that percents that are larger than 100 will convert to numbers that are greater than 1. So, when you divide 126.65 by 100, the answer is 1.2665.

Writing a number as a percentage relates to the way you write it as a decimal or fraction. A percentage that is less than 100 represents a number that is less than 1. A percentage that is greater than 100 represents a number that is greater than 1. A percentage that is exactly 100 represents a number that is exactly equal to (the same as, precisely) 1.

Here are some examples using percentages to figure out (calculate) how much extra you might pay in sales taxes, how much you might pay in income taxes, and how much you might earn in a savings account. Each example also shows the amount written as a percentage and as a decimal. You must convert percentages to decimals before you multiply or divide, or your answer will be very wrong. In fact, if you are multiplying, your answer will be 100 times too large, and if you are dividing it will be 100 times too small!

For example:

- You just bought a used car for $14,000. The sales tax where you live is 7%. You must pay an additional (extra) $980 in sales tax. This is usually paid at the point of sale, at the place where you bought the item. In your home country, the sales tax (value-added tax, or VAT, or MOM) is often included in the price of the items you are buying. In America, the tax is almost never included in the posted (listed, ticketed, marked) price of items.
- You earn $800 in one week. This is your gross pay. Social Security tax is 7.65%, state income tax is 4%, and federal income tax is 15%. How much tax will be taken from your pay? The remaining amount is your net (or take-home) pay. The answer: Add the percentages, then multiply the total times (by) your gross pay. This gives you the total

amount of tax you will pay. In this example, *7.65% + 4% + 15% = 26.65%*. When you multiply 800 by 26.65%, the amount of tax taken from your check is: *$800 · 0.2665 = $213.20*. To find out how much of your pay you keep (take-home), subtract the total amount of your taxes from your gross pay. Your net (take-home) pay is: *$800 – $213.20 = 586.80* per week.

- You have $4,000 in a bank savings account. This account pays 2% interest per year. How much money will your $4,000 earn (make) in one year? Answer: Multiply $4,000 by 2%. In other words, $4,000 · 0.02 = $80 per year. If you want to know the total value of your savings account after one year, you need to add the earnings—$80—to the $4,000 you started with. So, at the end of one year you will have $4,080. Next year, the entire value—$4,080—will earn 2%. This means you will get a bit more than $80 in interest the second year. This is called "compounding."

Converting decimals to percentages is simple (easy, basic). Just multiply the decimal by 100, or simply move the decimal point two places to the *right* and add the percent (%) symbol. So it is the exact opposite process you use when converting percentages to decimals.

If you need to convert a fraction to a percentage, you need to divide the top (numerator) by the bottom (denominator). This will give you a decimal. Be very careful to put the decimal point in the right place! Now you can convert the decimal to a percentage by multiplying by 100, or by moving the decimal point two places to the *right* and adding the percent symbol. Take a look at sidebar 3.2 to help you decide if a fraction will have a whole-number component (after you reduce the fraction).

When you convert decimals to percentages, the process is actually very simple. Figure 3.16 tells (shows, explains) how.

Converting Fractions to Decimals

- If the numerator (top number) is larger than the denominator (bottom number), the decimal will have a whole-number component.
- If the numerator (top number) is smaller than the denominator (bottom number), the decimal will not have a whole-number component.

Sidebar 3.2

3.1.6 Practice Exercises

Converting Decimals to Percentages

Convert the following decimals to percentages. Note that some of the decimals include whole numbers and some do not. Remember to move the decimal point two places to the right or multiply by 100.

a. 0.987 ______
b. 3.983 ______
c. 10.50 ______
d. 0.45 ______
e. 0.875 ______

Answers:

a. 98.7%
b. 398.3%
c. 1050% (The final zero is dropped because it is not necessary.)
d. 45%
e. 87.5%

Converting Percentages to Decimals

Convert the following percentages back to decimal form. Some of the answers will also include whole numbers. Remember to move the decimal point two places to the left or divide by 100.

a. 93.75%
b. 67%
c. 365%
d. 23.765%
e. 4250%

To convert decimals to percentages, multiply by 100. To convert percentages to decimals, divide by 100.

Figure 3.16 Converting Decimals to Percentages

Answers:

a. 0.9375
b. 0.67
c. 3.65
d. 0.23765
e. 42.5 (Note the zero at the end is left off—it is not needed in the decimal form.)

Converting Fractions to Percentages

Convert these fractions to percentages. Remember that this is a two-part (two-step) process. First you have to divide the numerator by the denominator, then multiply the result by 100. Be careful with the decimal points, too.

a. 3/5 ______________________________
b. 4 1/8 ______________________________
c. 7/8 ______________________________
d. 1.01 ______________________________
e. 5.985 ______________________________

Answers:

a. 60%
b. 412.5%
c. 87.5%
d. 101%
e. 598.5%

Practical Exercises

1. You get paid every Friday. You make $750 per week, before taxes. Social Security taxes on your gross pay are 7.65%. State income tax takes another 3% of your check (the amount you are supposed to be paid). Federal income taxes each week are 13% of your total pay.

a. What is the amount of your gross pay? ____________
b. Write the Social Security tax amount as a decimal. ____________
c. How much do you pay each week in Social Security taxes? ____________
d. How much do you pay in state income tax? ____________
e. How much do you pay each week in federal income tax? ____________
f. What is the total amount of your deductions each week? ____________
g. What is your net (take-home) pay? ____________
h. There are 52 weeks in a year, so how much is your gross pay (the amount before you pay taxes) each year? ____________
i. How much is your take-home (net) pay each year? ____________
j. How much do you pay each year in federal income taxes? ____________
k. About (approximately) how much do you earn in gross pay each month? ____________
l. Approximately (about) how much is your take-home (net) pay each month? ____________

2. You have invested $10,000 in bank certificates of deposit (CDs). You are earning 5% interest each year. At the end of one year you have earned $500.

a. How much money do you have after one year? ____________
   Now, if you put your $10,000 and the interest it earned into another CD paying 6% interest per year:
b. How much interest will you earn with this new CD? (Don't forget to add last year's $500 to your original $10,000!) ____________
c. How much money will you have now?

Answers to Practical Exercises:

1.

a. $750
b. 7.65% = 0.0765

c. $750 · 0.0765 = $57.38
d. $750 · 0.03 = $22.50
e. $750 · 0.13 = 87.50
f. $97.50 + $22.50 + $57.38 = $177.38
g. $572.62 ($750 − $177.38)
h. $39,000 (750 · 52)
i. $29,776.24 (572.62 · 52)
j. $5,070 ($97.50 · 52)
k. $3,250 ($39,000 ÷ 12)
l. $2,481.35 ($29,776.24 ÷ 12)

2.

a. $10,500
b. $630
c. $11,130

3.1.7 Other Numbers

Sometimes you will need to write numbers such as temperatures, directions (azimuths), and so forth in words. The same basic rules you just learned still apply.

When you write temperatures in words, you still hyphenate numbers between 21 and 99, except for 20, 30, 40, 50, 60, 70, 80, and 90. In addition, you need to add *degrees Fahrenheit* after the number for ASM temperatures and *degrees centigrade* for metric temperatures. The symbol (abbreviation) for degrees Fahrenheit is °F. The symbol for degrees centigrade is °C.

For example:

- 31°F is written as thirty-one degrees Fahrenheit.
- 22°C is written as twenty-two degrees centigrade.

3.2 IN THE REAL WORLD: WRITING A CHECK

As part of your day-to-day activities, you are probably going to write checks to pay bills, rent, tuition, and more. You don't want to be cheated when you write a check. You also don't want an incorrectly written (filled out) check to make your payment late. This means you need to correctly fill out your check.

In this chapter you are learning about writing actual numbers in words. You will need to be able to write the exact amount of the check in both numbers and words. If you make a mistake, your check might "bounce," meaning the bank won't accept it, or someone might be able to change what you wrote and cheat you. Figure 3.17 shows you a sample check. Most checks will be very similar to this example.

When you are writing a check, there are some important things you must do. There is also important (critical, key) information that must be preprinted (already) on your check.

[1] Your name must be preprinted on your checks. Your bank or the check-printing service does this for you. You can have more than one name here—yours and your spouse's, for example. Only the person or persons whose names are on the check are allowed to sign the check. The name should be printed just (exactly) as you will sign the check. If this is a business check, the business name and information is preprinted on the check. Only the person or persons in the bank's records may (is allowed to) sign the checks. Business checks are written the same way as personal checks. This example is a personal check.
[2] Your address also must be preprinted on your check. Many people also put their telephone number since merchants (sales clerks) ask for it. This is not always a good idea. You can always write your phone number on the check at the time you fill out the rest of the check. When

Name [1] Date ______________[4]
Address [2]
City, State, Zip Code [3]

[5]Pay to the order of ______________________ Amount __________[6]
Amount in words ______________________________________[7]

[8] Memo (reason)__________ Signed ______________________[9]

Figure 3.17 Sample Check

you need to provide your telephone number, it is a good idea to give your business (office) number rather than your home (personal) or cell phone number.

[3] Your address needs to be complete. That means you must include your city, state, and zip code. It is not necessary to include your country (USA).

[4] You must write the correct date. A check without a date or with the wrong (incorrect) date may be refused by the clerk or the company you send it to. If you make a mistake, correct it and put your initials next to the correction. When we change to a new year, people make lots of mistakes dating their checks!

[5] This is the only person, shop, or organization able to cash (get money from your bank for) this check. If the name (payee) does not fill the space, draw a line from the end of the name to the end of the space for the name. This name is called the "payee" and is indicated by the words "pay to the order of" preprinted on your check.

[6] This is where you write the actual amount of the check. This is written in numbers. Don't forget to write this amount and the "pay to the order of" person or place in your check register (record)!

[7] This is very important. You have been studying how to write whole numbers and decimals (and fractions) in words. This is the space where you must actually do this. Normally you write the whole number portion of the amount in words, and the decimal part as a fraction. So if your purchase amount is $123.76, you write $123.76 in the block marked with the [6], and then you write:

one hundred twenty-three and 76/100

in the space marked with the [7]. If the amount written in words does not fill the space, draw a line to fill the remainder of the space. This makes it harder for someone to alter (change) the amount you wrote.

[8] You don't usually have to fill in (write in) this section, but it is the best place to write your account number when you are using a check to pay a bill. This allows (helps) the payee (pay to the order of name) to know where to apply the check. It also helps to write a reason so you can manage your expenses later (see chapter 6, section 6.1, "Building a Budget").

[9] This block is also essential. Unless you sign your check, it is not valid (not good). The signature must match one of the names in [1] or in the bank's records for a business check.

Safeguard (protect) your checks. *Never* leave them in your car or anywhere someone can easily find them. Always fill out each check completely. If you make a mistake, destroy the check, and make a note (write the word "VOID") in your check register (checkbook).

Always write down the information for each check in your check register as soon as you write the check. Make sure you subtract the amount of each check from the total money in your account. "Bouncing" a check (writing a check when you know you don't have enough money) is a very bad idea. Even if you made an honest math error, you can still get into trouble. Your bank will charge you a lot of money ($20 to $50 or more) for each check that bounces. In some cases, you might end up in court and then in jail for writing a "bad" check. When your check bounces, it will be returned to you and be marked *NSF* (not sufficient funds).

You may want to use a software program such as Quicken or QuickBooks to record your checks and even to print them.

3.3 HOMEWORK: WRITING NUMBERS IN WORDS AND WORDS IN NUMBERS

Your homework is very important. The concepts in this chapter are simple and you use them every day. The reason you need to do homework is to get used to these concepts in another language. The more you practice, the easier it will be to do things correctly when it matters (counts).

3.3.1 Writing Actual Numbers in Words

Write the following whole numbers in words. Be careful to put any hyphens in the correct place. Not all the numbers will have a need for hyphens. Do not use "and" to connect the numbers. Practice saying each number. Look at the Word/Number Conversions Chart (table 3.1) if you are not sure when to use hyphens. Do not use "and."

1. 17 ____________________
2. 37 ____________________
3. 82 ____________________
4. 90 ____________________
5. 101 ____________________
6. 170 ____________________
7. 124 ____________________
8. 297 ____________________
9. 3,004 ________________________________
10. 4,096 ________________________________
11. 6,333 ________________________________
12. 11,201 ________________________________
13. 15,674 ________________________________
14. 19,005 ________________________________
15. 76,380 ________________________________
16. 101,456 ________________________________
17. 356,896 ________________________________
18. 407,700 ________________________________
19. 561,802 ________________________________
20. 3,456,999 ________________________________
21. 8,000,401 ________________________________
22. 7,400,396 ________________________________
23. 14,976,334 ________________________________
24. 34,567,900 ________________________________
25. 64,400,454 ________________________________
26. 124,333,898 ________________________________

3.3.2 Changing Numbers Written in Words to Actual Numbers

Note: Don't forget to put any commas in the right places!

27. Thirteen __________
28. Twenty-seven __________
29. Ninety __________
30. One hundred forty-three __________
31. Five hundred seventeen __________

32. Seven hundred four ____________
33. Five thousand sixty-seven ____________
34. Three thousand six hundred ninety-seven ____________
35. Twelve thousand five hundred fifty-five ____________
36. Thirteen thousand four hundred six ____________
37. Eighty-one thousand three hundred twelve ____________
38. Sixty-three thousand one ____________
39. Four hundred twenty-one thousand six hundred thirty-one

____

40. One hundred thousand ninety-one ____________
41. Two hundred ten thousand four hundred ____________
42. Five million two thousand seventeen ____________
43. Seven million three hundred thirty-three thousand four hundred

____

44. Eight million five hundred seven thousand sixty-three

____

45. Forty-four million seven hundred sixty-two thousand five hundred twenty-seven ____________

3.3.3 Decimals and Fractions Written in Words

Write the following decimals and fractions in words. Be careful to put any hyphens in the correct place. Not all the numbers will have a need for hyphens. Sometimes you will need to use "and" to connect the numbers. Practice saying each number.

46. 4/5 ____
47. 356 3/4 ____
48. 5 354/1,000 ____
49. 8 1/8 ____
50. 356 3/16 ____
51. 5.902 ____
52. 0.78654 ____
53. 98.9898 ____
54. 0.000098 ____
55. 34.010888 ____

3.3.4 Percentages Written in Words

Write the following percentages in words. Be careful to put any hyphens in the correct place. Not all the numbers will have a need for hyphens. Sometimes you will need to use "and" to connect the numbers. Practice saying each number.

56. 77% ______________________________
57. 143% ______________________________
58. 17% ______________________________
59. 3,461% ______________________________
60. 5.2% ______________________________

3.3.5 Converting Percentages Back to Decimals

Write the following percentages as decimals and whole numbers (if necessary).

61. 77% ______________________________
62. 143% ______________________________
63. 17% ______________________________
64. 3,461% ______________________________
65. 5.2% ______________________________

3.3.6 Converting Fractions to Percentages

Change the fractions below to percentages. Remember to multiply by 100 after you divide.

66. 4/5 ____________________
67. 1 2/3 ____________________
68. 1/2 ____________________
69. 2 1/4 ____________________
70. 423/978 ____________________

3.3.7 Other Numbers Written in Words

Write the following temperatures in words. Practice saying each answer.

71. 65° F ____
72. 22° C ____

3.3.8 Converting Decimals and Fractions Written in Words Back to Numbers

Write the following decimals and fractions in numbers. Be careful to put any hyphens in the correct place. Not all the numbers will have a need for hyphens. Sometimes you will need to use "and" to connect the numbers. Practice saying each number.

73. Two one thousandths ________________
74. Five and seventeen ten thousandths ________________
75. Four and three quarters ________________
76. Two thousand seventy-six and three thousand four hundred eighty-seven one hundred thousandths ________________
77. Ninety-eight and five sixteenths ________________
78. Two million one hundred seven thousand six hundred twenty-one and thirty-three one hundredths ________________
79. One half ________________
80. Seventy-one and thirty-three one hundredths ________________
81. Five sixty-fourths ________________
82. Ninety-nine one thousandths ________________

3.3.9 Converting Percentages Written in Words Back to Numbers

Write the following percentages in numbers. Watch out for decimal points and commas. Practice saying each number.

83. Four hundred sixty-three percent ________________
84. One thousand percent ________________
85. Sixty-two point five percent ________________
86. Eighteen percent ________________
87. Ninety-four percent ________________

3.3.10 Converting Other Numbers Written in Words Back to Numbers

Write the following temperatures in words. Practice saying each answer.

88. Twenty-five degrees Celsius ________________
89. Seventy-five degrees Fahrenheit ________________

3.3.11 Real-World Word Problems

Fill out the check using the information in the next problem. Don't forget to sign the completed check and provide (put) the correct date! If you make a mistake, initial any corrections you need to make.

90. Michaela Smets is going to pay her public service bill for her heat and electricity. The utility (in this case, gas and electric) company is Public Service of the East. The date is March 22, 2006. Michaela lives at 134 Main Street in Devonville, Massachusetts (MA), and her zip code is 99999 (note that this information has been filled in for you). Her bill (the amount she must pay) is $123.47. Her public service account number is 305–999–001. Use this information to fill out the check (see figure 3.18) below.

91. Rashid just received his paycheck for the month. Here is a copy of his "earnings statement" (see figure 3.19).

a. What (how much) is Rashid's gross (total) monthly pay? ________
b. How much (what amount) does Rashid pay in taxes? ________

Michaela Smets
134 Main Street
Devonville, MA 99999

Date ________________[4]

[5]Pay to the order of ____________________ Amount ________[6]
Amount in words ____________________________________[7]

[8] Memo (reason)________ Signed ____________________[9]

Figure 3.18 Practice Check

Monthly Earnings for Rashid Khan	Period: October 2006
Gross Pay	$4,000
Federal Withholding Tax (15%)	$600
Social Security Tax (7.65%)	$306
State Tax (5%)	$200
City Tax (3%)	$120

Figure 3.19 Earnings Statement

c. What percent (%) of Rashid's total (gross) pay does he pay in taxes?

____

d. What (how much) is Rashid's net (take-home) pay? ________________

(The correct answers follow chapter 6.)

4

Fractions, Decimals, Ratios, and Percents

We looked at some basic aspects (parts of) fractions, decimals, and percents in chapter 3. In this chapter you will learn more about fractions, decimals, percents, and ratios. You use all four of these mathematical tools (concepts) nearly every day.

4.1 FRACTIONS

When you see a number written as a fraction, you are seeing a shortcut that shows the relationship between two numbers. As mentioned in chapter 3, you have a numerator (the top part) and a denominator (the bottom part).

Fractions also indicate (show) that you could divide the denominator into the numerator. The result (answer) would be a decimal. This decimal will have a whole-number part (component) if the fraction was greater than 1. Take a look at sidebar 4.1 for some examples.

Cents and Fractions

- When you write a check, you are converting a decimal—the "cents" part of an amount—to a fraction.
- In the amount $123.47, you are converting the decimal portion (47) to a fraction.
- The equivalent fraction is 47/100 since there are 47 cents or forty-seven hundredths in the decimal portion.

Sidebar 4.1

Many times you will need to change fractions to a decimal form, especially if you need to convert to a percentage. Figure 4.1 shows you how to do this.

You use fractions every day. When you look at the fuel (gas) gauge in a car, the dial is normally divided into eighths or quarters. If your gasoline indicator (gauge) shows 3/4, you probably do a quick bit of math to figure out how much fuel is left in your gasoline tank. If your tank holds 16 gallons, you probably think "I have 3/4 (3 quarters) of a tank of gas. That means I have 3/4 of 16 gallons, or about 12 gallons left." Why would you bother to do this calculation? Maybe you think fuel prices are going to go up (rise) in the next week, and you know you have to drive 300 miles in that week. You also know your car gets 28 miles to the gallon. So, you should be able to drive 336 miles without filling up the tank (although it is always a good idea to fill the gas tank before it is empty!). Maybe you're just curious about how economical your car is—how much fuel it uses.

4.1.1 Multiplying Fractions

The preceding (earlier) example actually shows you the basic approach to multiplying when fractions are involved (used, present). There are a few

- The fraction 5/8 (written as five eighths) indicates you can divide 5 by 8. It also indicates you have 5 of 8 pieces, or 5 parts of every 8 parts. If you perform (do) the division, you get 0.625. The value of 5/8 is less than 1, so there is no whole-number part (component).
- The fraction 14/3 (written as fourteen thirds) is equivalent to (the same as) 4 2/3. This fraction has a whole-number component since its value is equal to or greater than 1. You can either divide 14 by 3, or you can find the whole-number part and divide the remaining numerator by the denominator. In this example, the whole-number portion (part) is 4, and the remaining fraction is 2/3, so you need to divide 2 by 3, and add the result to the whole number. In this case, 2 divided by 3 (2 ÷ 3) is about 0.67. When you add that to 4, you get 4.67. (Note: Since the actual result of dividing 2 by 3 is 0.6666666 . . . we rounded the 6 in the thousandths place to the nearest hundredth.) If you divided 14 by 3, you would also get 4.67.

Figure 4.1 Changing Fractions to Decimal Form

simple rules you need to know. Multiplying fractions is much easier than adding them, as you will see in section 4.1.3. Dividing fractions is also fairly easy, and is covered in section 4.1.2. Subtracting fractions is also not straightforward and is covered in section 4.1.4. There are a few simple rules, as figure 4.2 illustrates (shows).

Keep in mind the Commutative Property of Multiplication (see chapter 1). You can multiply fractions in any order. You can also multiply three or more fractions together by extending the process in figure 4.2. If you have three fractions, convert (change) any whole-number portions so you have pure fractions, then multiply all the numerators (tops) together and all the denominators (bottoms) together. The resulting fraction needs to be reduced (simplified) to its whole number and fractional components. (See sidebar 4.4 on page 86.)

The same approach applies for additional numbers of fractions. If one or more of the terms (components) you need to multiply is a whole number without a fractional component, put a 1 as the denominator for each whole number. Convert any fractions with whole-number components. Now you have all (pure) fractions and can multiply the numerators together and multiply the denominators together. Again, reduce the answer to a whole-number component and a fractional component if the answer (result) is 1 or larger (greater).

4.1.2 Dividing Fractions

Dividing fractions by other fractions or by whole numbers is almost the same as multiplying them together. The main consideration is to change the division problem into a multiplication problem. This is much easier than it sounds (seems, appears).

In section 4.1.1, you learned why putting a 1 as the denominator of a whole number makes the multiplication process easier. This same trick helps even more when you need to divide fractions by whole numbers. Here's an example to show you why putting a 1 in the denominator for whole numbers is so useful (see figure 4.3 on page 86; see also sidebar 4.5 on page 88).

So, division is really just a version (form, type, variation) of multiplication when you're working with fractions. Here's one more example, this time with two fractions with whole-number components. Figure 4.4

Before You Begin

- Convert any fractions that include a whole number to a "pure" fraction. For example, the fraction 5 1/2 would become 11/2 (since 5 is the same thing as 10/2). As another example, the fraction 13/4 is already in the correct form.
- Note that 5 is also the same thing as 5/1 since any number divided by 1 is unchanged (stays the same). You will see why this is important in the next steps.

Multiplying a Whole Number and a Fraction

- When you are multiplying a whole number and a fraction together, first convert the fraction to a pure fraction if necessary. If the fraction has a whole-number component, you will need to convert it to a pure fraction.
- When writing the whole number, put a 1 in the denominator.
- Now you can multiply the fraction and the whole number together.
- Multiply both numerators (tops) together.
- Multiply both denominators (bottoms) together.
- The resulting fraction can be simplified (reduced) if its value is greater than 1.
- For example, to multiply 3/4 and 5 together, you don't need to convert the fraction—it does not have a whole number component.
- Write the 5 as 5/1.
- Multiply the 5 and the 3 together (the numerators) to get 15.
- Multiply the 1 and the 4 together (the denominators) to get 4.
- The answer is 15/4. This answer is greater than (more than, larger than) 1.
- Rewrite 15/4 so it has a whole-number component and a fractional component that is less than 1.
- Divide 15 by 4 (15 ÷ 4). You get 3, plus a fractional component of 3/4.
- The final answer is 3 3/4 (written as three and three quarters).
- If the fraction contains a whole-number component and a fractional component, convert it to a pure fraction before multiplying the numerators or denominators.
- For example, to multiply 4 2/7 and 6 together:
- Convert 4 2/7 to a fraction: Multiply the 4 times 7 (the denominator), and add the result to the 2 in the numerator. Since $4 \cdot 7 = 28$, you now have the fraction 30/7. Check your work by converting 30/7 to a whole number and fractional component to make sure you get 4 2/7 (written as four and two sevenths) again.

- Write the 6 as 6/1.
- Multiply the numerators (6 and 30) together and the denominators (1 and 7) together.
- The answer is 180/7. This is much larger than 1, so you need to convert (reduce) your answer to whole-number and fractional components. Divide 180 by 7 (180 ÷ 7). You get 25 and a fractional component of 5/7.
- The final answer is 25 5/7 (written as twenty-five and five sevenths).

Multiplying Two Fractions Together

- Convert one or both fractions if they have whole-number components.
- Multiply the numerators together, then multiply the denominators together.
- Reduce the result to a whole-number component and a fractional component.

Figure 4.2 The Rules for Multiplying Fractions

Why Add a Denominator to a Whole Number?

- Adding a 1 as a denominator for any whole numbers that do not have fractional components is a simple trick that makes multiplication easier (simpler) because all the components look the same. Without the 1 in the denominator, you might miss a fraction or make a simple mathematical error.
- Remember that you can divide any number by 1 and the number is unchanged. Having a 1 in the denominator is equivalent to (the same thing as) dividing the number (numerator) by 1.

Sidebar 4.2

shows you the steps you need to follow (take) to divide one fraction by another fraction.

This is a good time to look at the Rule of Reasonableness as explained in figure 4.5.

4.1.3 Adding Fractions

The Commutative Rule of Addition still applies to fractions, but the actual process of adding fractions is not straightforward (simple, easy). In order

Converting Whole-Number Components to Fractions

- When a fraction has a whole-number component, you can covert the whole-number portion to a fraction by multiplying the whole number by the denominator. Then you add the result (answer) to the fractional component denominator and place the total over the denominator.
- Why does this multiplication process work?
- You can multiply any number by 1 and not change the number's value. When you multiply a whole number by the value of its fractional component's denominator, and then place the answer over the denominator, you have simply multiplied the whole number by 1.
- Consider the fraction 3 1/2. If you multiply the 3 by the denominator (2), and then place the answer (6) over the denominator, you are now able to divide the 6 by 2. In other words, you multiplied the whole-number component (3) by 2/2, and that is the same as multiplying by 1 (2/2 = 1).

$$3\ 1/2 = (3 \cdot 2)/2 + 1/2 = 6/2 + 1/2 = 7/2$$

- To check your answer, divide 7 by 2 (7 ÷ 2). You get 3, plus 1/2 or 3 1/2.

Sidebar 4.3

Multiplicative Inverses

- When you are multiplying two fractions together, and one is the exact opposite (inverse) of the other, the answer is *always* 1.
- Consider the example 2/3 · 3/2.
- When you multiply the numerators together (2 · 3), you get 6.
- When you multiply the denominators together, you also get 6 (3 · 2).
- Whenever you have a multiplication problem with two elements (terms) and the numerator of the first term is the same as the denominator of the second term, *and* the denominator of the first term is the same as the numerator of the second term, you know the result will be 1.
- Note that for this to happen, one fraction must be less than 1, and the other must have a whole-number component.

Sidebar 4.4

- You have 1 half (1/2) of a pie. You want to divide it into three equal pieces. How large will each piece of pie be?
- Dividing 1/2 by three is not that easy, but you can make this calculation simple by changing this problem into a multiplication problem.
- The process is called "invert and multiply." You "invert" (turn upside down) the divisor (the part that is doing the dividing). In this case, the divisor is 3 since you want to divide the pie into 3 equal pieces.
- Here is the problem before you change it into a multiplication problem:

$$1/2 \div 3 = ?$$

- First, give the 3 a denominator of 1.
- Now the problem becomes:

$$1/2 \div 3/1 = ?$$

- If this were a multiplication problem it would be simple, so let's change it into 1 !
- To make this a multiplication problem, you need to invert the divisor (the 3/1).
- Now the problem looks like this:

$$1/2 \cdot 1/3 = 1/6$$

- You just multiply the numerators together (1 · 1) and then multiply the denominators (2 · 3) together.
- The result: Each piece of pie is 1/6 (one sixth) of the original pie.
- Check your work: Multiply 1/6 by 3 (the number of pieces you cut the pie into). Give the 3 a denominator of 1, and the equation becomes:

$$1/6 \cdot 3/1 = 3/6$$

(3/6 can be reduced to 1/2.)

Figure 4.3 Dividing One Half of a Pie into Thirds

to add fractions, you need to convert all fractional components so they have the same denominator. You do not have to convert the whole-number components. You can add the whole-number components as you would in any ordinary addition problem.

So, how do you convert fractional components so they have the same denominator? There are two commonly used ways: Finding the least (lowest, smallest) common denominator, or finding any denominator that works. We are going to learn the second way. You will often get larger

Why Does Inverting and Multiplying Work?

- When you invert a fraction or whole number, you are actually multiplying each term by some number that makes the divisor equal 1.
- When you have 3/2 ÷ 2/3, you can simply invert the divisor (2/3) and change the problem to 3/2 · 3/2. Applying the rules in section 4.1.1, the answer is (3 · 3) / (2 · 2) = 9/4.
- This is the same thing as multiplying both terms by 3/2.
- Multiplying the divisor (2/3) by 3/2 will make the divisor equal 1.

$$2/3 \cdot 3/2 = 1 \ [(2 \cdot 3) / (3 \cdot 2) = 6/6, \text{ which equals } 1]$$

- As long as you do the same thing to the other term (the 3/2), you have not changed the problem. You can multiply anything you want by any number as long as you do exactly the same thing to every term in the equation.
- So, the first term becomes 3/2 · 3/2, which is the same as:

$$(3 \cdot 3) / (2 \cdot 2) \text{ or } 9/4$$

- Now you can multiply the two terms together:

$$9/4 \cdot 1/1 = 9/4$$

- This is the same result you got when you simply inverted the divisor and multiplied the two terms together.
- Another way to see (understand) why this works is to divide 2/3 by 2/3 (2/3 ÷ 2/3).
- Any number divided by itself is *always* equal to 1.
- Now invert the second term and multiply instead of dividing:

$$2/3 \cdot 3/2 = (2 \cdot 3) \div (3 \cdot 2) = 6 \div 6 = 1$$

Sidebar 4.5

numbers for your denominators, but you won't have to do a number of other steps.

To find a denominator that works, simply multiply each denominator value together. Figure 4.6 shows you the steps you need to (must) follow to find a denominator that works.

Next, adjust each numerator so the overall value of the problem stays the same. That means you are multiplying each numerator by the same number (or numbers) you used to increase (multiply) its denominator.

Divide 2 2/3 by 3 1/4

- First, convert both numbers to pure fractions since each one has a whole-number component.

$$2\ 2/3 = (6 + 2)/3 = 8/3$$
$$3\ 1/4 = (12 + 1)/4 = 13/4$$

- Now both terms (numbers) are in a form you can work with.
- Next, invert your divisor (13/4). The result is 4/13.
- Now you can multiply the two terms together instead of dividing them:

$$8/3 \cdot 4/13 = (8 \cdot 3) / (3 \cdot 13) = 24/39$$

- Check to determine (see) if the answer is equal to or greater than 1. Since it is less than one, you can only reduce it to a simpler fraction. In this example, you can divide both the numerator and denominator by 3. The simplified fraction becomes:

8/13

Figure 4.4 Dividing One Fraction by Another Fraction

Multiplying Fractions

- Remember that division of fractions can be made into a form of multiplication!
- When you are multiplying two fractions that are each less than 1, your answer must be less than 1.
- When you are multiplying two fractions that each have whole-number components, your answer must be greater than 1.
- When you are multiplying three or more fractions and all the terms are less than 1, your answer will be less than 1.
- When you are multiplying three or more fractions and all of the terms have a whole-number component, your answer must be greater than 1.
- If you have "mixed" terms—where some terms are less than 1 and some are greater than 1—be careful. There is no good rule, so you need to carefully check your answer.

Figure 4.5 The Rule of Reasonableness

- If you have two terms to add together, multiply the two denominators together.

$$2/3 + 7/12 = ?$$

- Multiply $3 \cdot 12$ to get 36. This is a denominator that will work. It is not the only denominator that will work, but it is easy (simple) to calculate (find).

A denominator that works is 36.

- Once you have a denominator that will work, you need to adjust your numerators.

Figure 4.6 Finding a Denominator that Works

This is equivalent to (the same as) multiplying each term by 1. In the example in figure 4.6, you multiplied the denominator of the first term (2/3) by 12 (to get 36), so you must multiply the numerator by the same amount. For the second term, you multiplied the denominator by 3 to get 36, so you must multiply the numerator by the same amount. Take a look at figure 4.7. This is another version of "multiplying by 1" (in this case, 12/12) to make a problem easier to manage.

If you are adding numbers (terms) where one or more terms had a whole-number component, you can simply add the whole numbers and then add the result to your answer from the fractional components. If the example in figures 4.6 and 4.7 were changed to:

$$2\ 2/3 + 3\ 7/12$$

you would add the 2 and the 3, and proceed to adjust the fractional component exactly as in figures 4.6 and 4.7. When you reach (obtain, get) the answer for the fractional components (1 1/4), you would then add the whole-number components ($2 + 3 = 5$) to the 1 1/4. So your answer would be:

$$1\ 1/4 + 5 = 6\ 1/4$$

If you are adding three or more fractions, the approach is the same, but the denominator will become much larger. As with the example in figure 4.6, you need to find a denominator that works, so you must multiply all

- In figure 4.6, you multiplied the denominators together to get a common denominator (a denominator that works). Now you need to make sure you adjust the numerators so the overall value of your answer does not change.
- Using the same example:

$$2/3 + 7/12 = ?$$

- In the process of finding a denominator that works, you decided to use 3 · 12, or 36.
- To keep the problem the same, multiply the numerator of the first term by 12 (the same number used with the denominator).
- The first term becomes:

$$(2 \cdot 12) / (3 \cdot 12) = 24/36$$

- To check your math, you can always reduce the term (24/36) and you will get your original term (2/3).
- Next, adjust the second term. Since its denominator was multiplied by 3 (12 · 3 = 36), its numerator must also be multiplied by 3:

$$(7 \cdot 3) / (12 \cdot 3) = 21/36$$

- Again, you could reduce the adjusted term and you would get 7/12.
- Now both terms have the same denominator, so you can add the numerators (not the denominators!) and place the result over the adjusted denominator:

$$24/36 + 21/36 = \frac{24 + 21}{36} = 45/36$$

- Note that the answer is equal to or greater than 1, so you need to separate out the whole-number component. The answer is:

$$1\ 9/36 \text{ or } 1\ 1/4$$

Figure 4.7 Adjusting the Numerators

the denominator values together to get the new denominator. Then you must multiply each numerator by the new denominator value, with one important exception. You must reduce the amount when you multiply the numerator—by dividing the new denominator by the value of the old denominator for each term—before you multiply the numerator. Figure 4.8 shows you the steps to take (follow) when you need to adjust the denominator and numerator when adding three or more terms.

Add: 5/6 + 1 2/3 + 3 1/2

- First, pull out any whole-number components, in this case 1 + 3. Don't forget to add this part to your fractional component answer!
- Next, find a denominator that works. Multiply each denominator value together.

$$6 \cdot 3 \cdot 2 = 36$$

- Now, adjust each numerator.
- For the first term, 5/6, divide the new denominator by 6 (the current denominator). Multiply the numerator by the result:

$$36 \div 6 = 6$$

- Multiply the numerator by 6:

$$5 \cdot 6 = 30$$

- The first term thus becomes:

30/36

- Check to make sure you did the multiplication and division correctly. Reduce the term 30/36. You get 5/6, so this term is adjusted correctly.
- For the second term, divide the new denominator by its current denominator (36 ÷ 3 = 12) and then multiply the numerator by the result (12):

$$2 \cdot 12 = 24$$

- The second term becomes:

24/36

- Again, a quick check by reducing the term gives 2/3, so this term is adjusted correctly.
- Repeating the process for the third term, the numerator needs to be multiplied by 18 (36 ÷ 2 = 18). This gives (18 · 1 = 18) so the third term is:

18/36

- As always, check your answer by reducing the term.
- So, the three adjusted terms (before adding the whole-number components) are:

30/36 + 24/36 + 18/36

- Combining these terms over the adjusted denominator, you get:

$$\frac{30 + 24 + 18}{36} = \frac{72}{36} = 2$$

- Now you can add back the whole-number components you put aside at the beginning (1 + 3 = 4) so your final answer is:

$$2 + 4 = 6$$

Figure 4.8 Adjusting the Denominator and Numerator: Three or More Terms

4.1.4 Subtracting Fractions

Subtracting fractions uses the same processes as adding fractions. First you have to find a denominator that works. Again, multiply the denominator values together to get a common denominator that will work. Remove the whole-number components, but pay attention to whether there was a plus (+) or minus (−) sign in front of the whole-number and fractional component. Then proceed to adjust your numerators and denominator exactly as for adding fractions. When you are done and have checked your adjusted fractions, perform the subtraction. Figure 4.9 shows you the steps to take to subtract fractions. It is similar to the process for adding fractions, but remember that the Commutative Property of Addition does not apply.

Signs are very important in subtraction. When in doubt, construct a number line to make sure you are moving in the correct direction. This is especially important if the equation combines addition and subtraction. Remember, there is no Commutative Property of Subtraction, so the order of operations matters.

4.1.5 Practice Exercises

Multiplying Fractions: Section 5.1.1

Multiply the following fractions. Remember to convert the whole-number portion and then multiply numerators together and denominators together. Reduce (simplify) your answers.

a. 6 3/4 · 5/3 = ____________________
b. 3/8 · 4/7 = ____________________

Subtract: 4 1/2 − 2/3

- Remove the whole-number component, but don't forget to consider it when you are ready to subtract the adjusted fractional components!
- Next, find a denominator that works:

$$2 \cdot 3 = 6$$

- Now, adjust each numerator:

$$1 \cdot 3 = 3$$
$$2 \cdot 2 = 4$$

- So, the adjusted terms become:

3/6
4/6

- Reconstructing (re-creating) the equation (including the whole-number component), you have:

4 3/6 − 4/6 = 4 + (3/6 − 4/6) = 4 + (−1/6) = 3 5/6

Figure 4.9 Subtracting Fractions

c. 9 2/3 · 3 3/11 = ________________
d. 1/2 · 3/8 = ________________

Answers:

a. 135/12 reduced to 45/4
b. 12/56 reduced to 3/14
c. 1044/33 reduced to 348/11
d. 3/16 does not reduce

Dividing Fractions: Section 5.1.2

Divide the following fractions. Remember to convert the whole-number portion. Don't forget to invert the divisor and make each problem a multiplication problem. Reduce (simplify) your answer.

a. 5 1/4 ÷ 3/8 = ________________
b. 7/8 ÷ 9/16 = ________________

c. 3 1/4 ÷ 1/4 = ________________

d. 9 2/7 ÷ 2 4/9 = ________________

Answers:

a. 21/4 · 8/3 = 168/12 reduces to 14

b. 7/8 · 16/9 = 112/72 reduces to 1 40/72 and further reduces to 1 5/9

c. 13/4 · 4/1 = 52/4 reduces to 13

d. 65/7 · 9/22 = 585/154 reduces to 3 123/154

Adding Fractions: Section 5.1.3

Add the following fractions. Don't forget to find a denominator that works and adjust each numerator. Pull (take) out the whole numbers and add them at the end.

a. 2/3 + 1/2 = ________________

b. 5 3/5 + 6 4/7 = ________________

c. 3 3/11 + 4/3 = ________________

d. 1/3 + 3/5 + 1/4 = ________________

Answers:

a. 4/6 + 3/6 = 7/6 reduces to 1 1/6

b. 5 + 6 + 21/35 + 20/35 = 11 + 41/35 reduces to 11 + 1 6/35 = 12 6/35

c. 3 + 9/33 + 44/33 = 3 + 53/33 reduces to 3 + 1 20/33 = 4 20/33

d. 20/60 + 36/60 + 15/60 = 71/60 reduces to 1 11/60

Subtracting Fractions: Section 5.1.4

Subtract the following fractions. Don't forget to find a denominator that works and adjust each numerator. Some answers may be negative numbers.

a. 3 5/6 − 7/8 = ________________

b. 2/3 − 1/6 = ________________

c. 9/16 − 1 4/5 = ______________________________

d. 9 3/7 − 6 4/5 = ______________________________

Answers:

a. 3 + (40/48 − 42/48) = 3 + (−2/48) = 2 46/48 = 2 23/24
b. 12/18 − 3/18 = 9/18 reduces to 1/2
c. 45/80 − 144/80 = −99/80 reduces to −1 19/80
d. 9 − 6 + (3/7 − 4/5) = 3 + (15/35 − 28/35) = 3 + (−13/35) = 2 22/35

4.2 DECIMALS

You use decimals every day. Change is given in dollars (whole numbers) and cents (a form of a decimal). Grocery store prices are in dollars and cents. Unit pricing, which is the cost per ounce or pound or other unit of measurement, is in decimal form.

A decimal is just a more precise version of a whole number. If everything were priced in dollars without cents, it would be easier to figure out your bill in a restaurant, grocery store, or other store. But you would probably spend a lot more money. Retailers (shop and restaurant owners) would almost certainly round all their prices up, not down.

When you are working with small numbers, the decimal component is important. In the laboratory, where results are measured in tenths of ounces, in grams, or even in milligrams or picograms, the decimal component is critical. When you are making a cake and measuring in cups and teaspoons, the decimal portion is not very important. Grade point averages are often calculated with a decimal component in order to differentiate (separate) the top students.

It is possible to be too precise. If you are adding several whole numbers and then dividing the result by another whole number (as is the case for grade point averages), having more than one or two decimal places has no real meaning (value, use). There is an entire category of mathematics devoted to "significant numbers." For practical purposes, you don't need (want) more than one or two decimal places more than you had in the original numbers. In other words, if the original numbers had no decimal places, you should not have more than 1 or 2 places when you are finished multiplying or dividing. If the original numbers had five decimal places, you shouldn't have more than 6 or 7 when you are done.

The rules of rounding are the way you decide whether or how to get rid of some decimal places. Take a look at figure 4.10 for the rules for rounding decimals when dividing.

Since you only started with whole numbers, to have more than 1 or 2 decimal places is of no real value. If you had started with:

$$2.2 \div 3.3$$

you already have one place to the right of the decimal point in each number. Your answer could have 1, 2, or even 3 decimal places:

$$2.2 \div 3.3 = 0.7$$
$$2.2 \div 3.3 = 0.67$$
$$2.2 \div 3.3 = 0.667$$

- If you are dividing 2 by 3 [2 ÷ 3], the answer is 0.6666666666666666 . . .
- A number with that many places after the decimal point is meaningless since you had only whole numbers to begin with.
- If you want one number after (to the right of) the decimal point, you need to start with two numbers to the right of the decimal point. Then you can round up or down.
- If you want two numbers to the right of the decimal point, you need to start with three numbers to the right of the decimal point. Then you can round up or down.
- In other words, you always need one more number (to the right of the decimal point) than you want to have when you have finished (completed) the mathematical operation(s).
- In this example, if you want one number to the right of the decimal point, you would start with 0.66 and round it to 0.7. If you want two numbers to the right of the decimal point, you would start with 3 numbers (0.666) and round to 0.67.

Figure 4.10 Rounding Decimals: Division

In each case, you still need to apply the Rules of Rounding.

There are many times when you would not apply the Rules of Rounding with decimals. For example, when you buy something, the price has two numbers to the right of the decimal point. Those numbers may be "00." Stores in America rarely round their prices up or down. In other countries rounding may be normal, but not here. If you buy items costing $2.33, $0.99, $23.00, and $4.44, your total cost is:

$$\$2.33 + \$0.99 + \$23.00 + \$4.44 = \$30.76$$

This amount is not rounded up to $30.80 or $31, even though those numbers would be easier to work with.

When you are multiplying numbers with decimal components, your answer will have more numbers to the right of the decimal point than any of the numbers you are multiplying together. Normally you should round your answer so you have no more than 1 or 2 more decimal points than the original number with the most numbers to the right of the decimal point. (See sidebar 4.6.)

What are the rules when you are multiplying numbers and want to round the decimal portion? Take a look at figure 4.11.

When you are adding or subtracting numbers with decimal components, it is a good idea to add zeros to the right of the last number following the decimal point if the numbers do not have the same number of digits to the right of the decimal point. This makes it less likely that you will make a simple addition or subtraction error. When you are adding or subtracting numbers with decimal components, it is easy to make simple math errors. Figure 4.12 shows you how to avoid these mistakes. Of course, if you're using a calculator (and are very careful), you can skip this process!

4.2.1 Practice Exercises

Perform the mathematical operation and then write how many decimal places you think your answer should have.

a. $4 \div 6 =$ ____________________
b. $39.3 \div 4.77 =$ ____________________
c. $4.4 \cdot 5.6 =$ ____________________

How Many Decimal Places?

- When you multiply decimals together, your answer (before rounding) should have the same number of decimal places as the total number in each number you are multiplying.
  Example:

  $$3.44 \cdot 4.21 = ?$$

- The answer will have four decimal places since there are two decimal places in the first number and two in the second:

  $$14.4828$$

- It is possible that one or more of the numbers at the far right of the decimal will be zero. In that case, you can leave them off. Your answer still has the correct number of decimal places, but you don't need to keep the zeros (except for cents).
  Example:

  $$3.22 \cdot 4.5 = ?$$

- The answer will have three decimal places since there are two decimal places in the first number and one in the second:

  $$14.490$$

- Since the last decimal place is a zero, you can leave (drop) it off. The final answer becomes:

  $$14.49$$

- The original answer had three decimal places, but the final digit (0) was meaningless, so you can drop (get rid of) it. The fact remains that the initial answer had the same number of decimal places as the total decimal places of the numbers being multiplied together.
- This gives you a quick way to check your answer. If you don't have the right (correct, proper, exact) number of decimal places in your answer, you know you need to recheck your multiplication.

Sidebar 4.6

- If you are multiplying 3.4 · 2.2, the answer is 7.48. There is no reason to round this answer. If you choose to round it, you could round it to the nearest tenth (7.5) or the nearest whole number (7).
- If you are multiplying 2.2 · 3.2 · 7.4444, the answer is 52.408576. Depending on your needs, you should probably round the answer to the nearest hundredth (54.09) or thousandth (54.086). If this answer was for a chemistry lab class, where exact figures are required, you might not round it at all.

Figure 4.11 Rounding Decimals: Multiplication

- Add the following numbers:

$$3.6 + 4.77 + 8.765 + 2$$

- If you use a calculator, the problem is simple (unless you enter numbers incorrectly!). If you are adding on paper, it is better to write the numbers in a column (up and down, vertically) and put zeros to give each number the same number of decimal places:

3.600
4.770
8.765
2.000

- Now the numbers are nicely aligned (lined up) and simple to add.
- The answer is 19.135.
- The same basic process applies for subtracting.

Figure 4.12 Adding or Subtracting Numbers with Decimal Components

d. 20.05 · 14.55 = ________________
e. 30.5 − 21.76589 = ________________
f. 40.1 + 99 + 35.777 + 10 + 65.56 + 0.002 = ________________

Answers:

a. 0.6666666 . . . This number should only have one or two decimal places, so the answer is 0.66 rounded to 0.7, or 0.666 rounded to 0.67.

b. About 8.239 . . . This is okay, or you could round to 8.24.
c. 24.64 . . . This is fine as is.
d. 291.7275 . . . You should probably round this to 291.728 (thousandths) or 291.73 (hundredths).
e. You would not normally round your answer when subtracting. 30.50000 − 21.76589 = 8.73411 (It is easier to do this vertically.)
f. Set this up as a column:

40.1
99
35.777
10
65.56
0.002

Now it is easy to see why adding the zeros (0) as placeholders is so useful!

40.100
99.000
35.777
10.000
65.560
0.002

The answer is 250.439. Again, you would not normally round answers when adding numbers.

4.3 RATIOS

Ratios are another mathematical tool you use nearly every day. A ratio is used to show the relationship between two numbers. When you see an advertisement that reads "Buy Three Get One Free" or "Two for the Price of One," you are seeing a form of ratio.

In the first case (Buy Three Get One Free), the ad is not clear. Do you have to buy three to get the fourth item free? Or do you get one item free out of each three you buy? In the second case, the ratio is much clearer. If you buy two items, you only pay for one. Of course there are rules such as paying for the higher-priced item and getting the less expensive one for free. This is to keep (prevent) the store from losing money.

For the "Two for the Price of One" example, you can write the ratio as 1:1. For each single (one) item you buy, you actually get a second item, too. For each dollar you spend, you get another dollar of merchandise. The wording of the offer affects the way you write the ratio.

A ratio of 1:1 (1 to 1) means that for each time the first thing (event, purchase) happens (takes place), a second event also happens. So the ratio of free to paid merchandise in this example is 1:1. You could also say that for each two items, the ratio of total items to paid items is 2:1, or total items to free items is 2:1. You could also say the ratio of free items to total items is 1:2, or paid items to total items is 1:2.

If an airline has a special promotion such as "Fly 1,000 miles and get triple miles in your frequent flyer account," what does that mean? For every 1,000 miles you fly, you get 3,000 miles in your account. So the ratio of miles you fly to miles you earn is 1,000:3,000 (and this reduces to 1:3). If you are already getting double miles (two [2] miles for each mile you fly, or 1:2) and the airline offers you triple miles as a special promotion, the ratio of miles flown to miles awarded (earned) is a bit tricky. You are already getting credit for the actual miles you fly, plus the same number of miles as part of the double miles promotion. If you are offered triple miles, the actual miles you fly are already included. You don't get credit twice. So, you get your actual miles flown, plus your double miles bonus. Then you get triple miles, but you have to subtract your actual miles since they aren't counted twice. So the final ratio of miles flown to miles awarded is 1:4, not 1:5. If you want the ratio of miles awarded to miles flown, you need to reverse the numbers (4:1).

Another example of a ratio you use every day is fuel consumption. If you use 10 gallons of gasoline (fuel) to drive 250 miles, that is 25 miles per gallon of gasoline. That means your fuel economy ratio is 1:25, or one gallon of gas for each 25 miles you drive. If you want the ratio of miles driven per gallon of gas used, the ratio is reversed (25:1).

Odds at the betting track or in a casino are another example of a ratio. If your odds (or chances) of winning something are 1 in 100, that means there will be 1 winner and 99 losers for each 100 times something happens. So the ratio of winners to losers is 1:99. If the odds of rolling a single dice and getting a 6 are one in six, then one roll will win and five will not. The odds of getting a 6 are one in every six rolls, but the ratio of 6s to other possibilities (1, 2, 3, 4, or 5) is 1:5.

The probability and statistics chapter (chapter 5) and examples in chapter 6 will explain more about likely outcomes at the casino, with board games (Yahtzee, Monopoly), predicting the weather, and so forth.

4.3.1 Practice Exercises

a. If there are 36 possible combinations from rolling 2 dice, what is the likelihood you will roll a 12? What is the ratio of your chances of rolling a 12 to your chances of rolling something else?
b. If your car will travel 350 miles on one tank of gas, and your tank holds 12 gallons of fuel, what is your fuel mileage? What is the ratio between 1 gallon of gas and the number of miles you can drive? (Note: Fuel mileage does not have to be a whole number; ratios can also have decimal components.)

Answers:

a. You have 1 chance in 36 of rolling a 12. There is a 1:35 ratio of 12 to other possible outcomes. Note that if you are considering the likelihood of rolling a 7, there are more chances since 6 combinations of the dice will give you a 7, but only two 6s will give you a 12.
b. 29.17 miles per gallon. Ratio is 1:29.17

4.4 PERCENTS

We looked at several examples that use percents to calculate taxes in chapter 3. Now let's consider (look at) other ways you use percentages in your daily life.

Percentages are just a more efficient way of expressing decimals, fractions that have been converted to decimals, or ratios. Figure 4.13 shows you examples of one number written as a fraction, a decimal, a ratio, and a percentage.

When you get a grade on an exam (test), it may be written as a fraction

- Each of the following mathematical expressions has the same value:

  4/5
  80/100
  1:5
  0.80
  80%

- The form you use depends on your purpose or application: your situation, need, or use.

Figure 4.13 Fractions, Decimals, Ratios, and Percents

showing your number of correct answers divided by the total number of questions. So, if your test had 100 questions and you answered 88 of the answers correctly (right), your score would be 88/100. This is the same as 0.88 (decimal form) or 88% (remember to multiply the decimal form by 100 to convert to a percentage).

When should you convert a number to a percentage rather than leave it as a decimal, fraction, or ratio?

Test (exam) scores almost always make more sense if you convert them to percentages. This is especially true if the score is based on a number of questions other than 100. Figure 4.14 shows you how to convert test scores to percentages.

There will be situations where you need to convert between fractions and decimals and percentages. Take a look at figure 4.15 to see how to do this.

You also use percentages when figuring out how much of your income you pay in taxes and other deductions (fees, insurance, retirement savings) each month. If you make $17.50 per hour and work 45 hours in one week, your gross pay is $787.50 per week. If the deductions for federal, state, local, and Social Security taxes total $225.43, you are paying 225.43/787.50 or about 29% (0.29) of your total (gross) income in taxes. The ratio of your taxes to your pay is 225.43:787.50. The ratio of your taxes to your take-home pay is 225.43:562.07. The ratio of your total pay to your take-home pay is 787.50:562.07. It is very important to understand the question so that you get the right answer.

In the example we just considered (looked at), if you want to know

- If you scored 17 out of 21 on a test, a percentage is much easier (simpler) to understand. To convert this to a percentage, write "17 out of 21" as a fraction:

$$17/21$$

- Now you can divide 17 by 21 ($17 \div 21$) and you get:

$$17 \div 21 = 0.81 = 81\%$$

- This is far more useful than the score 17 out of 21.
- The same consideration applies when there are more than 100 questions.
- If you had 127 out of 180 questions answered correctly, your score would be:

$$127/180 = 127 \div 180 = 0.71 = 71\%$$

- Each answer has been rounded to two decimal places since greater precision is not needed (necessary).

Figure 4.14 Converting Test Scores to Percents

what percentage of your gross pay equals your take-home (net) pay, you could do one of two things:

1. Subtract the amount you pay in taxes from your total (gross) pay. Divide that amount by your gross pay. In this example, $787.50 − $225.43 = $562.07. Dividing 562.07 by 787.50 (562.07 ÷ 787.50), you get 0.71, or 71%. The percentage amount of taxes plus the percentage amount of your net (take-home) pay should equal 100. The two dollar amounts (that is, the amount of taxes and deductions plus the amount of your take-home pay) should equal your gross (total) pay (earnings).
2. Subtract the percentage you pay in taxes from 100. The answer is the percentage you take home. In this case, $100 - 29 = 71$, so your take-home pay is 71% of the total you earn. To find the actual amount of your net pay, convert 71% to a decimal (divide by 100), and multiply the result (answer) by your gross (total) pay. In this case, $71 \div 100 = 0.71$, and $0.71 \cdot 787.50 = 559.13$. (Note: The answers in these two examples are not identical. The numbers were

Percentages (Percents)

- Numbers expressed (written) as a percentage that is greater than 100 equal a number that is greater than 1.
- A number written as a percentage that is less than 100 equals a number that is less than 1.
- A number written as 100% is exactly 1.

Decimals

- A decimal without a whole-number component (part) is always equal to a percentage less than 100.
- A decimal with a whole-number part (component) is always equal to a percentage greater than 100.

Fractions

- A fraction without a whole-number component converts to a decimal that is less than 1. This means that the fraction converts to a percentage that is less than 1.
- A fraction with a whole-number component converts to a decimal that has a whole-number component. This means that the fraction converts to a percentage that is greater than 1.

Figure 4.15 Writing Fractions and Decimals as Percentages

found (derived) using a calculator that automatically rounds numbers with more than two decimal places. As you can see, rounding can cause minor differences.)

When you calculate how much money your savings will earn, you rely on percentages. If your bank account is earning (making) 3% interest per year, and you have $9,654 in your account, at the end of the year you will have earned 3% of $9,654, or 0.03 · $9,654. You will have an additional $289.62, for a total of $9,943.62. An easier way to figure out how much money you will have at the end of the year is to multiply the amount you are beginning with ($9.654) by 103% (1.03 in decimal form). This works because you are getting your original money (100%) plus 3% more. So, at the end of the year you would have 103% of $9,654, or 1.03 · $9,654 = $9,943.62. Since you are multiplying by a percentage that is greater (bigger, larger) than 100, your answer should be larger than the amount you started with.

Percentages are also important when figuring out how much a loan or credit card is costing you. If your credit card charges you 21% of the unpaid balance (amount you owe) each year, and your average balance is $2,000, you will pay about 21% of $2,000. To see just how much that is, convert 21% to a decimal and then multiply that number by 2,000. In this case, 21% = 0.21, and 0.21 · $2,000 = $420 per year. That's a lot of money!

If you are paying interest for a car loan from a secondhand car dealer, you need to know how much of the total you pay for your car is actually interest. If the car costs $10,000 and your monthly payments are $250, and you are paying for 48 months, the total cost for your car is really (actually) $250 · 48 = $12,000. That means you are paying $10,000 for the car and $2,000 for interest (to the car dealer). The interest on the $10,000 you borrowed is 20% (2,000 ÷ 10,000 = 0.2 = 20%). So, one dollar out of every six dollars you paid was actually interest. The ratio of car payment to interest was 5:1; the ratio of interest to car payment was 1:5. That's a lot of money for a car loan.

If you want to know whether you will qualify for a mortgage, you need to understand the ratios that mortgage lenders use to decide if you can afford the house payments. These ratios are expressed as percentages. In most cases, if your planned mortgage payment plus all other monthly debt payments is more than 33 to 36% of your gross (total) earnings (pay), you will not get a mortgage. You will have to find a less expensive home or pay off (get rid of) some of your debts. Figure 4.16 shows you how to approximate the amount of mortgage you are eligible (qualify) for.

In the example in figure 4.16, your total debt load (total expenses) is too high. You need to do one of three things in order to get a mortgage:

1. Make (earn) more money. Maybe your spouse can get a job. Your family needs to earn between $3,500 and $3,750 to qualify for (get) a mortgage with a $600 payment. If you earn $3750, $1,250 is 33% of your gross earnings. If you earn $3,500, $1,250 is about 36% of your total monthly pay.
2. Get a smaller mortgage. If you can't pay off some of your current loans and credit cards, you can only afford between $990 (33%) and

Monthly Gross Earnings	$3,000
Monthly expenses for debts	$250 car payment
	$200 credit card payment
	$200 student loan payment
Total debts	**$650 (22% of gross pay)**
Planned mortgage payment	$600 (20% of gross pay)
Total debt payments	$1,250 (42% of gross pay)

Figure 4.16 Rough Mortgage Payment Estimation

$1,080 (36%) of your monthly pay for debt payments. That only leaves between $340 ($990 − $650) and $430 ($1,080 − $650) for your mortgage.

3. Pay off some of your debts, starting with the credit cards. Every dollar you reduce your monthly debt load (payments) is $0.33 more you can use for your mortgage. This is usually the best choice. It also improves your credit rating (score) so you may qualify for (get) lower interest rates on all your loans and credit cards.

Percentages are an important part of everyday life no matter where you live. In chapter 6, we'll look at more ways in which percentages are important to you.

4.4.1 Practice Exercises

Convert the following to percentages. Remember that a percentage can be greater than 100.

a. 5/4 is the same as ___________%
b. If you get 1 out of 5 questions wrong, what percent did you get wrong (incorrect)? ___________%
   What % did you get right (correct)? ___________%
c. 0.987 is the same as ___________%
d. 4.5 is the same as ___________%
e. Your mortgage payment is $500 per month. Your gross pay is $1,500 per month. What percent of your total pay is used (needed) to pay your mortgage? ___________%

Answers:

a. 125%
b. 20% wrong, 80% correct
c. 98.7%
d. 450%
e. 33.33%

4.5 HOMEWORK: FRACTIONS, DECIMALS, RATIOS, AND PERCENTS

4.5.1 Section 4.1: Fractions

Multiplying Fractions

Multiply the following fractions together. When possible, reduce your answer to a whole number and fractional component. If possible, reduce the fraction to a simpler one (e.g., reduce 3/6 to 1/2, or 14/32 to 7/16).

1. 5/4 · 5/4 = ____________
2. 4/5 · 5/4 = ____________
3. 1 5/9 · 6/7 = ____________
4. 2/9 · 99 1/2 = ____________
5. 3 3/5 · 4 4/7 = ____________
6. 1/2 · 3/4 = ____________
7. 36 1/3 · 1/3 = ____________
8. 6/7 · 9/3 = ____________
9. 5 · 1/8 = ____________
10. 4 7/8 · 13 = ____________

Dividing Fractions

Divide the following fractions by changing the problem to a multiplication one. If possible, reduce the fraction to a simpler one (e.g., reduce 3/6 to 1/2, or 14/32 to 7/16).

11. 4/5 ÷ 4/5 = ____________
12. 17 ÷ 1/2 = ____________

13. 3 1/3 ÷ 6 1/6 = ____________
14. 3/4 ÷ 7/8 = ____________
15. 14 1/4 ÷ 7 1/8 = ____________
16. 7/8 ÷ 2 = ____________
17. 8 1/7 ÷ 6 1/9 = ____________
18. 1/4 ÷ 1/2 = ____________
19. 6 1/5 ÷ 8 = ____________
20. 1 ÷ 9/10 = ____________

Adding Fractions

Add the following numbers. Don't forget to make the changes to the numerators and denominators. If possible, reduce the fraction to a simpler one (e.g., reduce 3/6 to 1/2, or 14/32 to 7/16).

21. 4/9 + 7/8 = ____________
22. 4 3/4 + 4/5 = ____________
23. 5 + 7/8 = ____________
24. 1/2 + 5 3/16 = ____________
25. 1 1/2 + 3 1/6 = ____________
26. 7 1/2 + 4 1/2 = ____________
27. 19 3/4 + 3 4/7 = ____________
28. 6 1/8 + 4 2/3 = ____________
29. 4 1/2 + 3 1/3 + 5 1/2 = ____________
30. 6 1/8 + 9 1/3 + 1 1/2 = ____________

Subtracting Fractions

Subtract the following fractions. Don't forget to make the changes to the numerators and denominators. Your answer may be a negative number. If possible, reduce the fraction to a simpler one (e.g., reduce 3/6 to 1/2, or 14/32 to 7/16).

31. 3/4 − 1/2 = ____________
32. 4 4/7 − 1 1/2 = ____________
33. 5 − 1 1/2 = ____________
34. 7 1/8 − 8 1/4 = ____________

35. 4 4/29 − 3 1/2 = ____________
36. 3/39 − 1/13 = ____________
37. 4 1/8 − 6 3/8 = ____________
38. 1 3/4 − 1 1/2 = ____________
39. 2 1/3 − 1 1/2 − 7/8 = ____________
40. 8 − 6 1/6 − 1 1/2 = ____________

4.5.2 Section 4.2: Decimals

Perform the indicated operation (add, subtract, multiply, or divide). Round your answer to a reasonable number of decimal places.

41. 2.2 · 4.789 = ____________
42. 0.999 · 0.543 = ____________
43. 1.1 · 44 = ____________
44. 9.76 ÷ 4.2 = ____________
45. 0.922 ÷ 3.7 = ____________
46. 33.3 ÷ 17.02 = ____________
47. 666/999 = ____________
48. 0.333 · 0.0001 = ____________
49. 4.33 + 8.0098 + 17 + 55.555 + 1001.1 = ____________
50. 17.01 − 3.4444 − 0.099 = ____________

4.5.3 Section 4.3: Ratios

51. If there are 36 possible combinations from rolling 2 dice, what is the likelihood you will roll a 7? What is the ratio of your chances of rolling a 7 to your chances of rolling anything else?
52. If your car will travel 400 miles on one tank of gas (fuel), and your tank holds 20 gallons of fuel (gas), what is your fuel (gas) mileage? What is the ratio between 1 gallon of gas and the number of miles you can drive with that gallon? (Note: Fuel mileage does not have to be a whole number; ratios can also have decimal components.)
53. If your car will travel 275 miles on 1 tank of gas (fuel), and your tank holds 10 gallons of fuel (gas), what is your fuel (gas) mileage? What is the ratio between 1 gallon of gas (fuel) and the number of miles you can

drive with that gallon? (Note: Fuel mileage does not have to be a whole number; ratios can also have decimal components.)
54. Which car is more fuel-efficient (that is, gets better mileage from one gallon of gas): the car in question 52 or question 53? ________________

55. Which car will go a greater distance on one tank of gasoline: the car in question 52 or question 53? ________________
56. You see an offer for "buy 3 shirts, get 1 free."

a. What does this mean? ____________
b. How many shirts do you think you have to pay for to get 1 shirt free? ____________
c. What is the ratio between the number of shirts you get free and the number you have to pay for? ____________
d. What is the ratio of the number of shirts you get to the number you actually paid for? ____________
e. What is the ratio of the number of shirts you get to the number you got for free? ____________

4.5.4 Section 4.4: Percents

57. 8/5 is the same as ________%.
58. If you get 3 out of 20 questions wrong, what percent did you get wrong (incorrect)? ________%
What percent did you get right (correct)? ________%
59. 0.4567 is the same as ________%.
60. 0.303 is the same as ________%.
61. 2/7 is the same as ________%.
62. If your ratio of correct to incorrect answers is 4:1, what percent did you get right? ________%
63. If your ratio of correct to incorrect answers is 6:2, what percent did you get wrong? ________%
64. 9.7 is the same as ________%.
65. If you earn 3.2% in your savings account and you have $10,500 to start:

a. How much interest did you earn over 1 year? __________
b. How much money do you have at the end of the year? __________

c. If you earn 4% the second year, how much interest will you get? (Remember to use your answer in b as the starting point.) __________

d. How much money will you have at the end of the second year? _____

66. 1 2/3 is the same as ________%.

67. Which is larger: 400% or 4.2? ________

68. Which is larger: 0.98765 or 98.765%? ________

69. Which is smaller: 4/6 or 65%? ________

70. Your mortgage payment is $630 per month. Your gross pay is $2,500 per month. What percent of your total pay is used (needed) to pay your mortgage? ________%.

(The correct answers follow chapter 6.)

5

Probability and Statistics

You use aspects (parts) of probability and statistics nearly every day. We are not going to get into the detailed applications of probability and statistics. Instead, we'll look at the general principles and how you can use these principles to estimate and make logical (reasonable) choices (decisions).

5.1 PROBABILITY

Probability is the mathematical term used when you try to decide how likely (possible) something is. You may want to decide if the weather report means it is likely to rain or snow. You may like to play card games, dice games, or slot machines and want to make better choices so you lose less money. You may play board games (Yahtzee, Monopoly, and so forth) and want to understand why you don't usually roll a 12 with the dice. Maybe you just want to understand what the weather expert means when he or she says there is "a 50% chance of snow" or "a 30% chance of rain showers."

5.1.1 Understanding Probability

The Weather

When you hear a weather report and the presenter (reader) says, "There is a 30% chance of light snow this afternoon," what does that mean? It doesn't mean there is a 30% chance it will snow in the entire country. It doesn't mean it will snow 30% of the afternoon in your city. It doesn't mean it will snow over 30% of the area that can hear the weather report.

A 30% chance of snow means the following: When conditions are just like they are today, it will snow about 1 out of every 3 times you hear this forecast (weather report). So, if the forecaster says there is a 30% chance of light snow for the next three days, on at least one of those days it will probably snow. If the prediction is for 2–4 inches of snow, one of those days will get that much snow, not each day in 30% of the city. You might want to put an ice scraper, gloves, and a blanket in your car!

So if your weather forecaster says there is a 50% chance of rain showers, and these showers are going to be heavy at times, that means that on 1 of every 2 days you hear this, it will rain. In fact, it will rain quite hard at times. It could rain the next five times you hear this forecast, then not rain at all the next four times, then rain the next seven times and not rain at all the next eight times. But, on average, it will rain, and rain heavily at times, one out of each two days you hear this forecast. It would be a good idea to take an umbrella with you!

Take a look at table 5.1 for some fictional (made up) weather predictions and actual weather.

Remember that a 50% chance (probability) of rain means that for similar conditions in a certain area, it will rain 50% of the days that get that forecast. In table 5.1, some days had a different prediction, so they are not

Table 5.1 Rain Predictions and Results

The weather forecaster predicted a 50% chance of thundershowers. Here are the days he was correct and incorrect.

June 3—right	July 7—right
June 7—right	July 10—wrong
June 8—wrong	July 11—right
June 9—right	July 14—wrong
June 11—wrong	July 15—right
June 14—wrong	July 17—right
June 15—wrong	July 19—wrong
June 18—wrong	July 22—right
June 21—right	July 24—right
June 23—wrong	July 27—right
June 27—wrong	July 30—right
June 29—wrong	August 1—right
June 30—right	August 2—right
July 2—right	August 4—wrong
July 4—wrong	August 6—right

on the chart. Between June 3 and August 6, the weather forecaster predicted a 50% chance of rain 30 times. That means it should have rained on about 15 of those days (half of them). How many days did it rain? Look at the "right" entries: 17 days. Therefore, it actually rained about 57% of the time. That is fairly close to 50%. In fact, if you had data for every time the forecaster predicted a 50% chance of rain, the results would probably be very close to 50%, meaning he or she was very accurate. Of course, that doesn't make you feel better when it rains on your party!

This brings us to how probabilities are actually determined. We rely on the Law of Large Numbers (figure 5.1) to validate statistical information.

Tossing a Coin

If you toss a coin 10 times, you could get all heads or all tails. You could get 5 heads and 5 tails. The data are not sufficient to draw a conclusion about the probability of getting heads or tails. At the same time, the fact that you tossed the coin and it landed heads up does not mean the next toss will be tails up.

If you toss a coin a few times, your pool (set) of results (data, statistics) is not enough (not sufficient) to draw conclusions. If you tossed a coin 100 times and got heads 65 times, it does not mean that the probability of tossing heads is 65% and tails is 35%.

If you toss a coin 10,000 times, you are going to have far more reliable data (statistics, information) . You will probably get 5,011 heads and 4,989 tails, or 4,887 heads and 5,113 tails, or similar numbers (results). In either example, the actual percentages round logically to 50%.

- If you base (do) your data collection on very large samples or populations, the results will be predictable.
- For example, if you toss a coin enough (many) times, and there are two choices—heads or tails—the results will be very close to 50% heads and 50% tails.
- If you only use a small sample, the results may not be accurate.

Figure 5.1 The Law of Large Numbers

In the first example, 5,011/10,000 = 50.11% and 4,989/10.000 = 49.89%. When you apply the rules of rounding to whole numbers, both results (answers) become 50%. In the second example, 4,887/10,000 = 48.87% and 5,113/10,000 = 51.13%. When you apply the rules of rounding to whole numbers, both answers become 50%.

A very interesting thing about the coin toss is that the result of one toss is completely independent of any previous or future tosses. This is because tossing a head one time does not remove the head from the pool of choices. It is right back there for your next coin toss. Sometimes a result reduces the pool and affects the future results. A good example is games involving a deck of cards.

Playing Blackjack or 21

When you play a card game such as 21 (also called blackjack), drawing (taking) cards reduces the choices (options) left in the deck. If there are 4 queens in a deck of cards, and you can see 3 of them on the table, the chances of getting that last queen have dropped dramatically.

5.1.2 Practice Exercises

a. If you are playing 21 and you can see two jacks on the table, do you think it is likely you will draw (get, be dealt) another jack? ______. Why do you think this? ______________

b. You and a friend are tossing a coin. Each of you tosses a quarter 100 times. You get heads 47 times and tails 53 times. Your friend says she got heads 28 times and tails 72 times. Which set of data is more likely to be accurate? ______________. Is it *possible* your friend could have thrown (tossed) the quarter and had those results? ____________ Is it *probable (likely)* she got those results? ______________. Do you think she made up (created, imagined) those results? ____________.

c. The weather forecaster has predicted a 50% chance of heavy snow for tomorrow. What does that mean? ______________________.
Should you cancel your plans to go hiking? ______________________.
Why or why not? ______________________.

Answers:

a. The chances are not high since there are so many other cards you could get instead of a jack. If you need (want) a jack, this is not good. If you need anything but a jack, the odds are very good (high).
b. Your results are very close to 50–50, so they are probably accurate. Your friend's results are so far from the expected result that they are not very likely at all. Perhaps the coin was altered (tampered with) to favor (cause) tails. Perhaps she made the numbers up. It is *possible* to get those results, but it is not *probable (likely)*.
c. On one of every two days with this forecast, it will snow. Of course, it may not snow for 5–6 days with this forecast, then it may snow for several days with this forecast, and so on. Over the course of a long period (such as a year), you can expect it to snow an *average* of one out of every two days with this forecast. If you don't mind hiking in the snow, by all means go, but be prepared for snow and bad driving conditions!

5.1.3 Using Probability

Probability allows you to make better guesses, choices, or decisions. If there is a high probability of rain each day for the next week (seven days), you may want to take an umbrella every day. If you are going on vacation and the seven-day forecast (prediction) is a 10% chance of rain each day, you may decide to take your chances and leave your umbrella home. On the other hand, if the forecast shows a 60% chance of rain almost every day for the entire week, you almost certainly want your umbrella. You may even want to go somewhere else for your vacation!

Making Sense of Games of Chance

A very practical application of probability is "games of chance": Yahtzee, poker, blackjack (or 21), roulette, craps, and other dice and card games. While each game has an element of skill, much of the outcome is based on chance or luck. Chance is actually determined by compiling (gathering, collecting) statistics and calculating (figuring out) probabilities.

The information and illustrations in this section are only approximate.

They are specific enough to help you make informed choices rather than lucky guesses. The information is not good enough for you to use to try and "beat the odds" to regularly make money at the casinos.

The likelihood (chance) of something happening when you take (choose) a card, roll dice, or pull the handle on a slot machine is fairly easy to predict (figure out). Take a look at tables 5.2 through 5.4.

Note that if you add the ratios in table 5.3, they add to 36/36. Probabilities must equal 1 or 100%, or you have made a mathematical error. Table 5.4 shows the two-dice combinations that are possible.

The pattern you can see is a bell curve. It is a symmetric pattern, shaped like a bell.

Tables 5.3 and 5.4 are numeric representations of dice. Figure 5.2 shows what each face (or side) of a die looks like: A die has 6 sides, as shown.

If you are playing a dice game and you need (want) to roll a certain combination, knowing the probability (likelihood, chances) of getting that combination may affect your decision about what to do next (what move

Table 5.2 Dice Odds: One Die*

Die Roll	1	2	3	4	5	6
Odds	1 in 6	1 in 6	1 in 6	1 in 6	1 in 6	1 in 6

*The singular of dice is "die." If you have two dice, each one is called a die.

Table 5.3 Dice Odds: Two Dice

Dice/Roll	*Odds*
1	Can't happen
2	1 in 36
3	2 in 36
4	3 in 36
5	4 in 36
6	5 in 36
7	6 in 36
8	5 in 36
9	4 in 36
10	3 in 36
11	2 in 36
12	1 in 36

Table 5.4 Possible Two-Dice Combinations

Roll a *1:*
Not possible with two dice

Roll a 2:
Die #1 = 1, Die #2 = 1
One possibility

Roll a 3:
Die #1 = 1, Die #2 = 2
Die #1 = 2, Die #2 = 1
Two possibilities

Roll a 4:
Die #1 = 1, Die #2 = 3
Die #1 = 2, Die #2 = 2
Die #1 = 3, Die # 2 = 1
Three possibilities

Roll a 5:
Die #1 = 1, Die #2 = 4
Die #1 = 2, Die # 2 = 3
Die #1 = 3, Die #2 = 2
Die #1 = 4, Die #2 = 1
Four possibilities

Roll a 6:
Die #1 = 1, Die #2 = 5
Die #1 = 2, Die #2 = 4
Die #1 = 3, Die #2 = 3
Die #1 = 4, Die #2 = 2
Die #1 = 5, Die #2 = 1
Five possibilities

Roll a 7:
Die #1 = 1, Die #2 = 6
Die #1 = 2, Die #2 = 5
Die #1 = 3, Die #2 = 4
Die #1 = 4, Die #3 = 3
Die #1 = 5, Die #2 = 2
Die #1 = 6, Die #2 = 1
Six possibilities

Roll an 8:
Die #1= 2, Die #2 = 6
Die #1 = 3, Die #2 = 5
Die #1 = 4, Die #2 = 4
Die #1 = 5, Die #2 = 3
Die #1 = 6, Die #2 = 2
Five possibilities

Roll a 9:
Die #1 = 3, Die #2 = 6
Die #1 = 4, Die #2 = 5
Die #1 = 5, Die #2 = 4
Die #1 = 6, Die #2 = 3
Four possibilities

Roll a 10:
Die #1 = 4, Die #2 = 6
Die #1 = 5, Die #2 = 5
Die #1 = 6, Die #2 = 4
Three possibilities

Roll an 11:
Die #1 = 5, Die #2 = 6
Die #1 = 6, Die #2 = 5
Two possibilities

Roll a 12:
Die #1 = 6, Die #2 = 6
One possibility

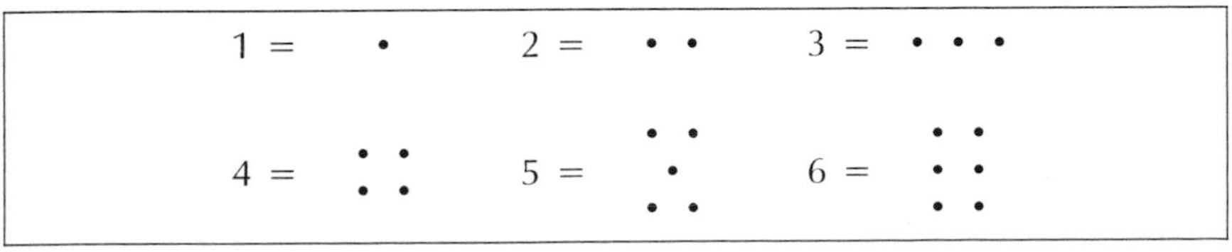

1 = •	2 = • •	3 = • • •
4 = ⁘	5 = ⁙	6 = ⠿

Figure 5.2 The Faces of a Die

to make). Since one roll of a pair of dice does not affect the next roll, you can't make a choice based on the rolls made by anyone else.

In the case of card games, cards that have been played (taken) are not normally replaced (put back) in the deck until the game is over. That means that the cards other players have taken will affect the cards you can get (draw).

5.1.4 Practice Exercises

a. If you are using one die, what is the likelihood (chance) you will roll a 4 on your first try?
b. If you are using one die, what is the chance (odds) you will roll a 3 on your third roll?
c. If you are using one die, what are the odds you will roll anything *except* a 5 on your 10th roll?

Answers:

a. 1/6
b. 1/6
c. 5/6

When you are playing card games, the odds (chances) of drawing (getting) a particular card will increase each time a different card is drawn (taken, dealt). On the first draw, you have an equal chance of getting any of the 52 cards in a deck, as shown in table 5.5.

Table 5.5 shows the odds of drawing a single card. If you are interested in the odds of drawing any card in one suit, the odds are 13 out of 52 (on the first draw) since there are 13 cards in each suit. That fraction reduces to 1 out of 4.

a. If you choose a card from a 52-card deck, what are your chances of getting (drawing) the ace of clubs? ______________________
b. You have drawn four cards from a 52-card deck. You have the ace of diamonds, the 7 of hearts, the jack of diamonds, and the 3 of spades. What are your chances of drawing the 2 of diamonds the next time? ____________

Table 5.5 Cards: Odds*

	Spades	*Clubs*	*Hearts*	*Diamonds*
Ace	1 in 52	1 in 52	1 in 52	1 in 52
Two	1 in 52	1 in 52	1 in 52	1 in 52
Three	1 in 52	1 in 52	1 in 52	1 in 52
Four	1 in 52	1 in 52	1 in 52	1 in 52
Five	1 in 52	1 in 52	1 in 52	1 in 52
Six	1 in 52	1 in 52	1 in 52	1 in 52
Seven	1 in 52	1 in 52	1 in 52	1 in 52
Eight	1 in 52	1 in 52	1 in 52	1 in 52
Nine	1 in 52	1 in 52	1 in 52	1 in 52
Ten	1 in 52	1 in 52	1 in 52	1 in 52
Jack	1 in 52	1 in 52	1 in 52	1 in 52
Queen	1 in 52	1 in 52	1 in 52	1 in 52
King	1 in 52	1 in 52	1 in 52	1 in 52

*Note that odds and ratios are not quite the same. The odds of drawing (getting) a particular (single) card are 1 in 52 since there are 52 cards. The ratio of the card you want to the remaining cards in the deck is 1:51, since there are 51 other cards in the deck.

Answers:

a. Since there are 52 cards, you have a 1 in 52 chance of drawing 1 specific (particular) card the first time. That is a ratio of 1:51 since 51 of the cards would not be the one you want.
b. Since you have drawn 4 cards, there are only 48 cards left (remaining). Your chances of drawing one specific card are 1 in 48. That is a ratio of 1:47 since 47 of the cards are not the one you want.

5.2 STATISTICS

Statistics are derived from (calculated from) data (information) in order to try and predict the future or determine a pattern. You may have heard the saying "Numbers don't lie." Well, statistics are numbers, and statistics can lie. It is possible to make statistics "say" (mean) almost anything. These false (misleading) statistics can be used to get some very strange results (answers). (See sidebar 5.1.)

Statistics are used to calculate or determine (figure out) probabilities. You will learn more about this in the following sections.

Lying with Statistics

Example #1:

- You are collecting information from a group of college students. There are 1,000 students in a lecture hall, and they all have agreed to take your survey about driving.
- The survey consists of one question with three choices:
- If the speed limit is 65 mph, at what point are you speeding (going too fast)?
- Choice #1: 66 mph
- Choice #2: 70 mph
- Choice #3: When the police stop you and say you were speeding.
- Here are the results:
- Choice #1: 100 agreed.
- Choice #2: 300 agreed.
- Choice #3: 600 agreed.
- In this example, 10% considered anything above the posted speed limit to be speeding. Another 30% considered more than 4 mph over the posted amount to be speeding. But 60% didn't consider themselves to be speeding unless a police officer (cop) said so.

Example #2:

- When the same question was asked to a group of 1,000 AARP members (people who are 50 or older), here are the responses:
- Choice #1: 10 agreed.
- Choice #2: 900 agreed.
- Choice #3: 90 agreed.
- In this example the results were very different. Only 1% felt anything over the limit was speeding. The vast majority—90%—felt that 4 miles over the limit was speeding. And only 9% felt that they weren't speeding until they were caught by the police.
- As you can see, the statistics vary greatly depending on the source of the data and the way the questions are asked. In this example, if you want to "prove" that speed limits are too low, you could use the data from the first poll (survey) and not tell anyone that the people who answered are very young.
- It's easy to twist (misread, misuse) data to make a point and claim that the results are based on "statistics."

Sidebar 5.1

5.2.1 Understanding Statistics

Statistics can be defined (explained) in many ways. The simplest (easiest) way is to consider statistics as a group of numbers that have been collected and organized. The numbers (data) are collected from a group of people, events, or other activities. The sources of the data must be related in some way, or the data are meaningless. Figure 5.3 gives an example of meaningful statistics.

Figure 5.4 gives an example of meaningless statistics.

5.2.2 Practice Exercises

a. Are the following data meaningful statistics? What could you do with the information?

- You want to know which fruits and vegetables will ripen most quickly if placed in a paper bag. You choose 100 bananas, 100 avocados, 100 tomatoes, 100 apples, and 100 oranges. You place each fruit in its own brown paper bag. You check each fruit or vegetable every morning to see if it is ripe yet. You record (write down) when each one is finally ripe.
- You have the same number and types of fruits and vegetables that you place on the counter (as controls). You check them each day to see how they compare to the bagged fruits and vegetables.
- If you chose fruit and vegetables that were all "green" (perhaps each type from the same plant), you will get some useful data. Some items will not ripen at all in the bags. Some items will ripen much more quickly.

Figure 5.3 Meaningful Data or Statistics

- You want to determine which type of fruit is the "reddest." You buy 100 apples, 100 oranges, 100 bananas, and 100 kiwis.
- You examine each fruit and decide the apples are the reddest.
- You tell everyone that "statistics show apples are the 'reddest' fruit."
- This is completely meaningless since it is very unlikely that any of the other fruits you chose will be red at all.

Figure 5.4 Meaningless Data or Statistics

You looked at (examined) 1,000 pieces of fruit. These fruits were divided into 150 red fruits, 300 yellow fruits, 400 purple fruits, and 150 green fruits. You also looked at 1,000 vegetables. These vegetables were 200 white vegetables, 700 green vegetables, 75 orange vegetables, and 25 black vegetables.

1. Is this meaningful information? ____________
2. In your experience, is this completely true information? ____________
____
3. What, if anything, could you do with this information? ____________
____

Answers:

1. The information is only meaningful (of value) if it is true (correct, accurate).
2. Fruits and vegetables come in many colors other than the ones listed in the exercise. The data are incomplete, so the statistics are not useful.
3. There is very little you could do with this information.

5.2.3 Using Statistics

Statistics are important in many aspects of academic life and in the rest of your life. Without accurate data (statistics), it is hard (difficult, not easy) to make good (informed, intelligent) decisions.

If you enjoy playing games of chance (cards, dice, slot machines), statistics are important because that is how the odds (chances) of winning are determined (calculated). If you want to get information about a new country, city, state, or other area, statistics are very important. Politicians (that is, elected and unelected officials) rely on statistics to decide how to spend money (taxes). Statistics are used to show the impact (effect) of a decision or to justify (explain) a decision.

One of the most useful sets of data (statistics) for living in America is the information about the area you live in. These same statistics can help you decide whether you want to move to an area (country).

Governments, chambers of commerce, and many other organizations collect lots of useful statistics. Some of the information you might find of use (value) is:

- Population: how many people live in a state, city, or other area.
- Average age of the population: If you are 65, you may or may not want to live in a city where the average or median age is 27! Note also that there is a difference between average and median.
- How many people live in 1 square mile: If there are thousands of people, that may mean many people live in apartments (flats). When people live in apartments, it is more likely there will be good public transportation. If there are hundreds, or fewer, people per square mile, that may mean houses are far apart (not close), and therefore there may be no public transportation.
- Educational level: If you are looking for a technology-based job, you are more likely to find one in an area where many people have a college degree.
- Schools: Many areas provide a large variety (range) of information about their schools. These data may include class size, test scores, graduation rates, and more.
- Weather information such as temperature ranges for each month, lowest temperature, highest temperature, annual precipitation (snow and rain), annual snowfall, and so on: If you are thinking of moving to Florida but you don't like hurricanes, you should look at the statistics about hurricanes in that state before you go. If you are thinking of moving to Montana and you don't like snow, you should look at the information about Montana's annual snowfall. If you like cool weather, the statistics will show (tell) you that much of Arizona is very hot (110°F in summer!). If you like water sports, statistics will show that there is not much water in New Mexico.

5.3 HOMEWORK: PROBABILITY AND STATISTICS

5.3.1 Understanding Probability

1. The weather forecast has predicted a 20% chance of rain showers for the past 13 days, but it has only rained (showered) twice. Today the fore-

cast is a 20% chance of showers. Do you think it will rain or not? ________. Why? ________________________________

2. If you choose a card from a 52-card deck, what are your chances of getting (drawing) the ace of clubs? ____________________

3. You have drawn four cards from a 52-card deck. You have the ace of diamonds, the 7 of hearts, the jack of diamonds, and the 3 of spades. What are your chances of drawing the 2 of diamonds the next time? ____________

4. If you choose a card from a 52-card deck, what are your chances of getting (drawing) the 10 of clubs? ____________________

5. You have drawn 6 cards from a 52-card deck. You have the 4 of diamonds, the 8 of hearts, the king of diamonds, the 5 of hearts, the 6 of clubs, and the 3 of spades. What are your chances of drawing the 5 of diamonds the next time? ____________

5.3.2 Using Probability

6. If you are using one die, what is the likelihood (chance) that you will roll a 3 on your second try? ____________________

7. If you are using 1 die, what is the chance (odds) that you will roll a 3 on your eighth roll? ____________________

8. If you are using 1 die, what are the odds that you will roll anything *except* (but) a 4 on your thirteenth roll? ____________________

9. If you are using 1 die, what are the odds you will roll anything *but* (except) a 3 or 6 on your fourth roll? ____________________

10. John rolled 1 die 10 times and got three 3s, two 4s, two 6s, one 1, one 5, and one 2. Do you think this is *possible*? ________________ Do you think it is *probable*? ________________ Why or why not? ____________________

11. Marta rolled 1 die 10 times and got a 5 every time. Is this possible? ____________ Is it probable? ____________ Why or why not? ____________

12. Explain why the odds of rolling a particular number do not change based on earlier rolls of 1 die. ____________________________

5.3.3 Understanding Statistics

Which of the following sets of statistics are meaningful? To be meaningful, you must be able to use the information in a practical way.

13. You are planning a vacation to Florida. You want to go when it is not too rainy and not too hot. You did some research and found the following. Number of days with at least 1/4″ of rain:

March: 7
April: 8
May: 7
June: 20
July: 15
August 8
September: 9

Number of days when the temperature is 85°F or warmer (higher):

March: 0
April: 4
May: 10
June: 19
July: 21
August: 24
September: 13

a. Is this useful information (statistics)? ____________________
b. Why or why not? ____________________
c. Which months are best for your trip? ____________________

(The correct answers follow chapter 6.)

6

Putting It All Together

You've read lots of mathematical information and even worked with some examples you will encounter (come across) in actual (real-world) situations. In this chapter, you will get to put all the pieces together to learn ways to help adjust to life in America. In section 6.1, you'll learn to make a budget. In section 6.2, you'll see how to estimate the costs of starting and owning a business. Section 6.3 explains how to plan a trip. Another useful skill is reading a map, and that is covered briefly in section 6.4. The remaining sections will help you read a compass, plan for retirement, convert a recipe, and more.

6.1 BUILDING A BUDGET

How do you know how much money you need to earn (make)? How do you know how much money you have to spend? How do you know if you can afford a new car or a better (nicer, bigger) apartment?

Simple. You make a budget (spending plan). A budget is just a spending plan—a list of everything you need or want to spend money on. This list includes your expenses and obligations: the things you *must* pay. Your budget also includes money for the things you *want*, but may not need. The other part of a budget is your income. Your income is usually your wages (salary).

What goes into your budget? What expenses should you list (include)? Keep this in mind: Budgets are normally made based on your expected expenses for a month. Most people get paid several times a month, and most bills are due once each month.

Some of the most common items you need to include are:

- Your monthly income (salary)
- Your rent or house payment
- Money for repairing and maintaining your home
- Money for your property taxes if you own a home
- Money for furniture and other décor to make your house or apartment nice
- Your income taxes
- Credit card payments
- Other loan payments
- Your insurance expenses—health insurance, car insurance, homeowner's or renter's insurance, and any other insurance you need to pay
- Your food expenses for meals at home
- Your expenses for meals at work and meals in restaurants
- Your car payment
- Your car expenses—maintenance, repairs, gasoline (fuel), parking, tolls (user fees), and so forth
- Money for clothes
- Money for entertainment (movies, books, travel, and so forth)
- Money for utilities—telephone, cable TV or satellite, Internet, heating, electricity, water, sewer, and so forth
- Money for child care (day care)
- Money for school (such as ESL classes, night school, and college)
- Money for yourself—haircuts, manicures, and so forth
- Money for savings
- Money for retirement
- Money for emergencies

As you can tell, there are many things you can spend money on. Some things are what we call "essentials"—you need these things to survive (live). Other things are nonessential, but still very important. These are the things that make living more fun. Rent or your mortgage payment is an essential. Renting movies is nonessential, but makes life more enjoyable (fun).

Saving money is important if you want to buy major (large) items, such as a car or refrigerator. By saving money to buy these things, you don't use your credit cards too much. Saving money is also important for emergencies, so that if your car breaks down (does not work) you have the money to fix it. Saving money for retirement is also important. In America, you are responsible for saving at least part of the money you will need for retirement. Our government does not pay as generously for retirement as many other governments do.

6.1.1 Practice Exercises

On a sheet of lined paper or graph paper, or on an accounting ledger:

a. Make a list of expenses for your budget.
b. If you think an expense is essential, place a check mark (√) next to it. Explain why this is an essential (necessary) expense rather than a nonessential expense.
c. What kind of emergencies should you plan for? How much money do you think you should save each month for emergencies? Make a list of at least 10 emergencies you should plan for. You may want to work with one or two other people to do this.

If you are a student, you need to plan for the time you finish school and get a job. You may not know how much money you need for rent, food, car payments, or other things. Someone else (such as your parents, scholarships, or your government) is probably paying your expenses now. But you need to know how much (how large) your salary needs to be when you graduate. This is a very good time to start learning how to "budget"—how to live with the amount of money you will earn (make).

Making (creating) a budget (spending plan) is not hard. You can look in the newspaper and see (learn) how much rent is for a small apartment. You can look at ad circulars (brochures) for grocery stores and furniture stores and other stores to see (learn) how much things cost. You can ask friends who already have apartments how much they pay for rent and utilities. You can ask your friends who have graduated how much they pay for insurance (health, auto, renter's, and so forth).

a. Read the local paper and find out how much rent, food, and other expenses in your budget cost. Make a list of these expenses, and put them in your budget.

b. Estimate how much money (salary) you need to pay these expenses. Don't forget to estimate how much your income taxes will be! (See chapter 2, "Estimating, Approximating, and Rounding," if you need help estimating these numbers.)

If you are already working or looking for work, you need to have a budget that fits your income. If you don't have a budget, you may think you are being paid a lot of money. Once you have a budget, you may discover (find out) that you are not earning (making) enough money. With a budget (spending plan), you will know how much money you need to earn (make) to buy the essential things you need and the nonessential things you want (like). Don't forget to include your income and the taxes you pay. Remember: Everything costs more than you expect!

a. Write out your budget in table 6.1.
b. If you need more money than you earn, write down your plan for earning this money. If you have been using credit cards to pay this shortfall (the difference between what you earn and what you spend), write down how you plan to pay your credit card debt.

Most people calculate their expenses (costs, bills) on a monthly basis. This makes sense since most people get paid at least once each month. Table 6.1 is a basic budget for you to use.

You can probably think of other things to add to this list—property taxes if you own a home, car license fees, and many other things. A category (line item) called "miscellaneous" is always a useful thing. Remember that unexpected items always add to your budget.

6.2 STARTING, BUYING, OR RUNNING A BUSINESS

Part of the American dream is often to own a business. Few things are as exciting, but also as risky (dangerous), as starting or running a business. Most people who fail as business owners do so for one or more of several reasons:

Table 6.1 Monthly Budget

Monthly Expense Item	*Cost of Item*
Rent or mortgage	
Utilities (heat, air conditioning, electric, gas, water, sewer, cable or satellite TV, Internet access, telephone, cell phone, pager, and so forth)	
Car payment	
Car expenses (gas, tolls, parking, maintenance and repairs, insurance, etc.)	
Other insurance (renter's or homeowner's, liability, health, life, disability, long-term care, etc.)	
Food	
Work expenses (meals, uniforms, dues, books, travel)	
Tuition, books, fees	
Holidays, vacations, and travel (airfare, hotels, rental cars, meals, entertainment, admissions, pet care, etc.)	
Personal care (haircuts, manicures, massages, health club memberships, etc.)	
Meals away from home, movies, videos, other entertainment	
Furniture, appliances, carpet, and so on	
Clothes	
Child care expenses	
General savings	
Emergency savings	
Retirement savings	
Miscellaneous	

- Choosing to start or buy a business that is not needed
- Choosing a business that they have no experience with
- Mismanaging their business
- Employee theft or turnover (quitting)
- Lack of money and planning

The last reason—lack of money and planning—is largely (mainly) solved by managing dollars (your money). That's what applied mathematics is all about.

So how can you plan and manage your money to increase the chances your business will succeed and grow? You need to have a financial plan. Just as you need a budget to manage your personal money, you also need a budget for your business money. There are many types of plans you need, but the most basic one is your "operating projection." Most banks want your operating projection to cover an entire year. If you decide to do your projection on a monthly basis, you will need to allocate (average) many of your payments over one year's time. This is also known as "allocating," and you will learn about it in the next section.

6.2.1 Allocating Expenses

Allocating expenses is a technique (method) to spread a payment made once a year, once every six months (semiannually), or every three months (quarterly) as a monthly payment. This allows you to save (put aside) a portion of a large payment every month so that you have the money when you actually have to pay a bill.

If you need to pay something once each year (such as property taxes), you allocate the payment by dividing the total amount due for the year by the number of months in the year. If you need to pay something twice each year (such as auto insurance), you allocate the payment by dividing the amount due every six months (semiannually) by six. If you need to pay something four times each year (such as water and sewer charges), you allocate the payment by dividing the amount due every three months (quarterly) by three. Figure 6.1 shows you several ways to allocate your expenses so you can budget for them each month.

Allocating Annual Expenses:

- If your annual property taxes for a business building are $2,400, you can allocate the total bill as monthly payments.

$$\$2,400 \div 12 = \$200$$

- It is much easier to put aside $200 each month so you have the entire $2,400 when you actually have to pay the tax bill.
- When you are tracking your expenses in the chart that comes later in this section, you can either enter (put) $200 each month for taxes, or $2,400 in the month the taxes are actually due (payable).

Allocating Semiannual Expenses:

- If your auto insurance payments are $720 every six months, you can allocate the semiannual bill as monthly payments.

$$\$720 \div 6 = \$120$$

- It is much easier to put aside $120 every month so you have the entire $720 when you have to pay the car insurance bill.
- When you are tracking your expenses in the chart that comes later in this section, you can either put (enter) $125 each month for auto insurance, or $720 in the month the taxes are actually due.

Allocating Quarterly Expenses:

- If your quarterly water and sewer bill is $300, you can allocate the quarterly bill as monthly payments.

$$\$300 \div 3 = \$100$$

- It is much easier to put $100 aside each month so that you have the entire $300 when you actually have to pay the water and sewer bill.
- When you are tracking your expenses in the chart that comes later in this section, you can either put $100 each month for water and sewer charges, or $300 in the month the payment is actually due.

Figure 6.1 Allocating Expenses

6.2.2 Calculating Your Business Operating Expenses

It is always a very good idea to try and decide how much money you need to earn to pay all your business expenses. Then you can figure out (calculate) how much money you need to pay yourself and also put money aside for new equipment or other charges (costs). Table 6.2 contains the information a bank wants if you are trying to get (qualify for) a loan from the Small Business Administration (SBA). It is basic, but makes a very good starting place. When you are thinking about starting a business, this table will help you ask the right questions to estimate your costs. If you have just started a business, this table will help you decide if you are making or losing money. If you are thinking about buying a business or franchise, table 6.2 will help you ask the managers the right questions.

Table 6.2 Operating Projection

Expense	*Month 1*	*Month 2*	*Month 3*	*Month 4*
Net Sales				
Cost of Goods Sold				
Gross Profit				
Depreciation				
Bad Debt Expense				
Bank Charges				
Telephone (basic, long distance)				
Internet (access and website)				
Satellite or Cable Charges				
Advertising and Marketing				
Dues and Fees (licenses, memberships, union)				
Equipment Rental (including lease payments for autos and trucks)				
Insurance (auto, property, liability, products and operations, health, life, disability)				
Loan Interest (SBA, bank, auto)				
Other Interest (credit cards, etc.)				
Office Supplies and Furniture				
Pensions and Employee Benefits				
Utilities (gas, electric)				
Rent or Mortgage				
Repairs and Maintenance				
Salaries and Wages—Staff				
Salaries—Officers and Owners				
Security (building and software)				
Taxes (payroll, state, federal, city, etc.)				
Taxes (sales)				
Licenses				
Other				
Total Expenses				
Operating Income (loss)				

You can easily create this form as a spreadsheet using Microsoft Excel or a similar program. Your tax advisor or banker can also give you this form. Programs such as Quicken also have the capability to develop this form. The chart above only shows four months, but you would need to project (calculate) your operating projections for an entire year. Otherwise you will overlook (forget) some important expenses that do not happen (occur, take place) every month.

What does each item in the chart mean? Take a look at figure 6.2 for explanations of each item in table 6.2.

When you are just starting a business, your operating projection will not be too complicated, but it is still essential. In the following practice exercises, you will actually work with the operating projection chart.

6.2.3 Practice Exercises

a. You are thinking about buying a franchise of a business. Go to your local library or bookstore and find a magazine that specializes in franchising, which is buying a business that is part of a chain of businesses, such as a McDonald's or a Jenny Craig Weight Loss Center. You can also do a search at www.google.com, entering "franchising magazine" in the search field. Some magazines to consider are:

- *Franchising Magazine*
- *International Franchising Magazine*
- *Successful Franchising Magazine*
- *Inc. Magazine*

Try to collect (find, gather) enough information to fill in table 6.3. If you can't find the information you need, try to estimate it or ask someone who owns a franchise or business to help you. There are also realtors (real estate agents) who specialize in selling franchises (or other businesses), and others who specialize in renting office space. They can help you estimate many of the costs. An accountant may also be able to help you estimate costs. The process for estimating the costs of owning a franchise (table 6.3) are almost identical to the process for calculating operating projections in table 6.2.

Do you think that your business idea will work? Is it affordable? Do

Net Sales: The total amount of your sales, less returns of previously sold products and credit for previous services.

Cost of Goods Sold: The cost of the materials and services used to make your product or provide your service.

Gross Profit: The difference in net sales and cost of goods sold.

Depreciation: The amount of tax deduction you are allowed to take for the reduction in value of your buildings, autos, trucks, and similar property.

Bad Debt Expense: Many times you sell something and the purchaser doesn't pay right away. This is especially true for services. After a certain number of weeks or months, these unpaid charges are considered "bad debts." You will probably never get paid for those items or services.

Bank Charges: Banks charge many fees, for bounced (bad) checks, monthly fees, ATM cards, and many other things.

Telephone (basic, long distance): You probably will have several telephone lines, equipment, long-distance charges, and toll-free calling. You probably also have a cell phone or two.

Internet (access and website): Few businesses even try to operate without these features. If you have a large site, you have design and maintenance charges, Internet service or hosting charges, and many other costs.

Satellite or cable charges: If you have these features at the office, they are business expenses.

Advertising and Marketing: You need a budget for printing, notices and flyers, newspaper ads, and marketing events.

Dues and Fees (licenses, memberships, union): Most professional organizations, unions, chambers of commerce, lead groups, and other organizations have fees for membership. You may also need professional licenses to practice your trade.

Equipment Rental (including lease payments for autos and trucks): If you lease vehicles for your business, or rent trucks or other equipment, this is where to allocate the costs.

Insurance (auto, property, liability, products and operations, health, life, disability): Insurance is a major expense for a business. You need many types to comply with laws, to protect your employees, and to protect yourself.

Loan interest (SBA, bank, auto): If you bought your business cars and trucks, you are probably paying for them with a loan. If you borrowed money from the SBA or a bank, you have interest payments.

Other interest (credit cards, etc.): Many new businesses can't get bank or SBA loans. Their owners use credit cards to pay everything. That usually means interest charges since the bills are not paid in full each month. You may also have credit cards for business purchases, travel expenses, and so forth.

Office Supplies and Furniture: You may need to buy furniture, and office supplies are an ongoing expense.

Pensions and Employee Benefits: You need to provide benefits such as health insurance and pension plans to hire and keep the best employees.

Utilities (gas, electric): You need power, heat, and light as well as water and sewer services.

Rent or Mortgage: You either rent or are buying the space where you have your offices. There is a cost for this.

Repairs and Maintenance: Everything seems to need to be fixed or maintained. You have vehicles, a building, forklifts, computers, software, concrete walkways, and much more.

Salaries and Wages—Staff: People expect to be paid. This is probably one of your biggest expenses.

Salaries—Officers and Owners: Owners also like to be paid, but this is an area you can reduce if you need to.

Security (building and software): You need to protect your physical buildings and equipment, control access to your site, and protect your data.

Taxes (payroll, state, federal, city, etc.): As an employer, the two fastest ways to get in trouble are failure to pay employees and failure to pay taxes.

Taxes (sales): If you sell a product, you have to collect sales taxes.

Licenses: Your city and state may have licenses you have to buy. You also have to buy vehicle licenses.

Other: Every business has unique expenses that aren't covered on standard forms.

Total Expenses: Add all the above expenses together.

Operating Income (loss): Subtract the total from your gross profit to get your projected operating income.

Figure 6.2 Explanation of Table 6.2: Operating Projection

Table 6.3 Estimating Franchising Costs

Expense	*Month 1*	*Month 2*	*Month 3*	*Month 4*
Net Sales				
Cost of Goods Sold				
Gross Profit				
Depreciation				
Bad Debt Expense				
Bank Charges				
Telephone (basic, long distance)				
Internet (access and website)				
Satellite or Cable Charges				
Advertising and Marketing				
Dues and Fees (licenses, memberships, union)				
Equipment Rental (including lease payments for autos and trucks)				
Insurance (auto, property, liability, products and operations, health, life, disability)				
Loan Interest (SBA, bank, auto)				
Other Interest (credit cards, etc.)				
Office Supplies and Furniture				
Pensions and Employee Benefits				
Utilities (gas, electric)				
Rent or Mortgage				
Repairs and Maintenance				
Salaries and Wages—Staff				
Salaries—Officers and Owners				
Security (building and software)				
Taxes (payroll, state, federal, city, etc.)				
Taxes (sales)				
Licenses				
Other (franchise fees and expenses)				
Total Expenses				
Operating Income (loss)				

you think a bank will lend you the money you need to get started? Why or why not?

b. You are thinking about starting your own business. Go to your local library or bookstore and find books and magazines that specialize in helping people start and grow businesses. You can also do a search at www

.google.com, entering "starting a business" in the search field. Some resources to consider are:

- *Startup Journal* (from the *Wall Street Journal*)
- The Small Business Administration's site for starting a business: www.sba.gov/starting_business
- *Inc. Magazine*
- The Internal Revenue Service business startup website: www.irs.gov/businesses/small/article/0,,id=99336,00.html

You can also do the same Google search, but include your state's name (for example, "starting a business California") to get state-specific information.

Try to collect (find, gather) enough information to fill in the table below. If you can't find the information you need, try to estimate it, or ask someone who owns a franchise to help you. There are also realtors (real estate agents) who specialize in selling franchises and others who specialize in renting office space. They can help you estimate many of the costs. An accountant may also be able to help you estimate costs. The costs to start up a business can also be estimated using the same approach as in table 6.2. If you are thinking of starting a business, make a copy of table 6.4 and see what your costs will be. You may have to estimate many of the items.

Do you think your business idea will work? Is it affordable? Do you think a bank will lend you the money you need to get started? Why or why not?

6.3 PLANNING A TRIP

One of the most exciting things about living in America is the ability to travel. As long as you have a car (or can rent one) or can use a recreational vehicle (also known as an RV or camper), you can travel across this vast country for a reasonable (moderate, affordable) amount of money. If you develop (make) a trip plan and budget, you can travel quite cheaply (inexpensively). It is easy to research costs, hotels, campgrounds, sights (at-

Table 6.4 Estimating Business Startup Costs

Expense	*Month 1*	*Month 2*	*Month 3*	*Month 4*
Net Sales				
Cost of Goods Sold				
Gross Profit				
Depreciation				
Bad Debt Expense				
Bank Charges				
Telephone (basic, long distance)				
Internet (access and website)				
Satellite or Cable Charges				
Advertising and Marketing				
Dues and Fees (licenses, memberships, union)				
Equipment Rental (including lease payments for autos and trucks)				
Insurance (auto, property, liability, products and operations, health, life, disability)				
Loan Interest (SBA, bank, auto)				
Other Interest (credit cards, etc.)				
Office Supplies and Furniture				
Pensions and Employee Benefits				
Utilities (gas, electric)				
Rent or Mortgage				
Repairs and Maintenance				
Salaries and Wages—Staff				
Salaries—Officers and Owners				
Security (building and software)				
Taxes (payroll, state, federal, city, etc.)				
Taxes (sales)				
Licenses				
Other				
Total Expenses				
Operating Income (loss)				

tractions), food, and other costs online. To find information online, just try www.google.com and enter "tourist information" and the name of the places you want to visit in quotes in the search box.

Now that you have all this information, what else can you do to manage the costs of your trip? You need to be practical and plan how far you will drive each day. Places are far apart in America!

You need to collect maps to help with your trip planning. Your local bookstore is a good source. If you are a member of an automobile association (club), you may be able to get free maps and trip-planning assistance. You may also be able to get free accommodation (hotel or campground) guides from the automobile club. Bookstores also have hotel and campground guides, as well as books about national and state parks and other attractions. How do you plan a trip?

6.3.1 Decide Where You Want to Visit and What You Want to See

First, you need to decide what places interest you. You could ask where your friends and coworkers suggest (recommend). You could look in a travel magazine and send away for information. You could visit a travel agent. You could do online and library research. You could look at the travel book section at a bookstore. You could see if an airline is offering great package (all in one) deals (specials) to a place that interests you.

Make sure the places you are considering have attractions and activities that interest you and your family or friends. If you like to water-ski, you may not find the Grand Canyon very interesting. If you are on a small (tight) budget, Palm Springs in California may be too expensive. If you want to camp or use a camper (RV), New York City may not be a good choice.

Once you have several places to choose from, you need to estimate your travel budget. You have two travel budgets—the amount of *time* you can spend and the amount of *money* you can spend.

6.3.2 Decide How Long You Can Travel and How Much You Can Spend

Your Time Budget

You probably can't spend several months traveling. Even if you could spend the time, you might not have the money to pay your expenses (costs) for that much time. Americans don't get as much paid vacation and holiday time (paid time off) as in most other countries.

America is a very big place. To drive from Miami, Florida, to Seattle, Washington, covers about 3,000 miles (what is that in kilometers?). More important, covering (driving) that distance takes *lots* of time. If you drove 500 miles every day (a reasonable amount if you don't plan to sightsee), it would still take six full days for the trip. You wouldn't get to see (visit) anything, either! That might be okay if you are moving to a new city and just want to get there (arrive). It doesn't make for much of a vacation (holiday), though. If you want to drive from Seattle, Washington, to San Diego, California, you are driving about 2,000 miles. It's a spectacular drive along the Pacific Coast, so you probably want to spend more than 4 days doing this.

You will hear Americans say, "It takes six days to drive there," not, "It is 3,000 miles between here and there." That's because distances here are so great (vast, far).

If you are planning to see the sights as you drive to places, you probably don't want to drive more than 200–300 miles most days. Some days you will just sightsee and not drive very far; other days, you may drive 500–600 miles just to get somewhere. You need to plan this driving schedule so you can build a budget for gas, accommodations, and meals; admissions to parks, zoos, and museums; and other costs. You also need this information to decide whether your planned trip is reasonable (doable). Figure 6.3 shows a possible driving and sightseeing schedule for a round-trip (circle tour) from Denver, Colorado, to Yellowstone and Grand Teton National Parks, with several other stops.

Driving 2,800 miles in 13 days means *averaging* over 200 miles per day, including the days you are touring (sightseeing). That's a lot of driving, and many of the roads you'll use are not fast (super, Interstate) highways. One of the key steps covered later is the difference in average speed for different types of highways. America has many marked (signposted) "scenic highways and byways" that are well worth driving, but they are not fast roads. They are narrow, two-lane roads across mountains and deserts or through canyons or small historic towns. These byways may even be dirt roads or require a 4-wheel-drive vehicle.

Your Monetary Budget

When you look at the driving schedule in figure 6.3, sometimes you will be able to camp, especially in or near the national parks (if you have a reservation!), but sometimes you may need or want to stay in a hotel or

- Driving from Denver, Colorado, to Yellowstone and Glacier National Parks
- Day 1: Drive from Denver to Yellowstone/Grand Teton National Parks in Wyoming. Estimate 500 miles. No sightseeing.
- Days 2, 3, 4, 5: Tour inside Yellowstone and Grand Teton Parks. Estimate 150 miles per day, 750 miles total.
- Day 6: Drive over the Beartooth Highway to Glacier National Park in Montana. Estimate 300 miles with a stop along the Beartooth Highway and a visit to Red Lodge.
- Days 7, 8, 9: Tour inside Glacier National Park. Estimate 100 miles per day, 300 miles total.
- Day 10: Drive from Glacier National Park to Blackfoot, Idaho. Estimate 400 miles.
- Day 11: Drive from Blackfoot, Idaho, to Dinosaur National Monument in western Colorado. Estimate 300 miles.
- Day 12: Tour Dinosaur National Monument and Grand Mesa, Colorado. Estimate 200 miles of driving.
- Day 13: Return to Denver, stopping at Glenwood Springs Hot Pool and Georgetown to ride the Loop Railroad. Estimate 250 miles of driving.
- Total driving: Estimate 2,800 miles.

Figure 6.3 Sample Driving Schedule

motel. You will be gone for 12 nights and 13 days. If you camp for the 8 days you are actually in national parks, that will probably cost about $15–20 per night. The other 4 nights, you'll probably be in hotels or motels (unless you have an RV or camper). These hotels and motels will probably cost about $50–75 for each room (one to four people in a room). Many hotels let one more child (five total people) stay in a room for an additional (extra) $10. They provide a cot (bed) for that child.

You'll need to buy food or eat in restaurants. If you shop and cook in your RV or over a campfire, you might spend $10 per person per day for food. If you eat in restaurants, you should estimate about $20–25 per person per day.

If your car gets (averages) 25 miles per gallon of fuel (gas) and you are going to drive about 2,800 miles, you will need 110–120 gallons of gas for the trip. If gas (fuel) costs $1.60 per gallon, that is a cost of $176–192 for fuel (gas).

You need to pay for national park admissions (you can buy an annual pass for about $75), admissions to the Glenwood Hot Springs Pool (about $15 per person), souvenirs, and food. Food can easily cost $25 per person per day, and may cost more, unless you are doing your own cooking.

So, let's estimate the basic costs of the trip in figure 6.3 for a family with four people. The numbers in figure 6.4 have been rounded up to avoid surprises later. Some costs include sales tax for hotels and food, so an extra 8% has been included.

6.3.3 Collect Travel Information

The Internet is a wonderful source of travel information. You can get detailed maps at www.mapquest.com, including driving directions. Another excellent source of travel information and maps is an automobile club such as AAA or Mobil. Many automobile clubs have arranged discounts

- There are five people traveling: 2 adults and 3 children.
- Driving 2,500 miles will cost about $200 for fuel.
- The National Parks Pass will cost about $75.
- It will cost $15 per person to go to the Hot Springs Pool, so that's $75.
- There are five people traveling, so hotels for 4 nights will cost about $370 ($75 + $10 for the cot), times 4 nights, plus 8% sales tax. The answer, $367.20, was rounded to $370. If you can find less expensive hotels, this amount will be less.
- Food in restaurants will cost $20–25 per person per day for the four days in the hotel plus the final day of traveling. That is $20 · 5 people · 5 days = $500 for the lower cost, or $25 · 5 people · 5 days = $625 for the higher cost.
- Caravan parks or campgrounds cost $15–20 per night. Assuming $20 per night for 8 nights, that equals $160.
- Food cooked at a campsite will cost about $10 per person per day for the 8 days you are camping. That is $10 · 5 people · 8 days = $400.
- Your research showed no costs for road tolls or bridge tolls.
- You might also add another $100–200 for emergencies and souvenirs.
- Total estimated trip cost: $200 + $75 + $75 + $370 + $625 + $160 + $400 + $200 = $2,105.

Figure 6.4 Trip Cost Estimates

(reduced prices) for their members for hotels and restaurants and campgrounds/RV parks.

6.3.4 Plan Your Route and Schedule

The maps you get online or from other sources contain a huge (very large) amount of information. It is important to find out if any roads will be under construction (being repaired) while you are on vacation there. Your automobile club should be able to tell you, or you can go to each state's website and find the information from the highway department or state patrol.

There is a *legend* on each map. This is a small chart that shows how far 1 inch (1″) on the map would be in actual miles. Many times, the legend also shows the number of kilometers in inches, too. This legend also shows the type of roads—interstate (4–6-lane) highways, state and U.S. highways (2–4 lanes, often with traffic lights), local roads, and dirt roads. They even show scenic roads. Most legends will show you symbols for highway *exits* so you can find them, and other codes to tell how far you have to drive between exits. Finally, you will see symbols for buildings, campgrounds, airports, historic sites, parks, and much more.

Maps often have "insets"—smaller maps of some of the cities in the area. These special maps show more detailed information such as local roads so you can find your hotel or campground.

Make sure you take into consideration the quality of the roads you have to drive on (4–6 lanes and no stoplights, or 2 lanes with lots of stoplights.) You may be able to average 60 mph on an interstate highway. You will be lucky (fortunate) to average 25–40 mph on a scenic highway, and you will average even less if you stop to sightsee or have a picnic (outdoor) lunch.

Spend some time looking at your maps and planning your route before you leave. Make sure the roads you plan to take (use) are open and not being repaired. Make reasonable (conservative) estimates about how far you will drive each day and what you will see. If you really read (understand) the legend, you will know the number of your exit from the highway, how far you must drive between exits, and what type of road you'll be driving on.

Your automobile club may design (make, create) a special trip map for you that shows the best or most interesting route. They can also mark road-repair areas, highlight the sights you want to see, and include city maps so you can find your hotel. These clubs often have guidebooks with city maps, touring information, and information about hotels and restaurants that are reliable (good quality and price).

6.3.5 Reserve Your Hotels and Campgrounds

If you plan to travel during the busy times of the year (summer, Christmas, Thanksgiving, or school holidays), you should reserve hotels, motels, inns, or campgrounds well ahead of time. Most places have toll-free (800, 888, 877, or 866) numbers so you don't have to pay for the call. Many places also have a website and e-mail address so you can preview the facilities (equipment, room, sites) and reserve by e-mail or the Internet.

Make sure that the places you plan to stay in (at) are easy to reach, not too far to drive to each day, and close to the places you want to see (visit).

6.3.6 Estimate Your Costs and Create a Budget

Figure 6.4 showed an estimate for the cost of a "circle" trip from Denver, Colorado, to Yellowstone and Grand Teton National Parks. Do some research to find a place you would like to visit, get maps and online or guidebook information, then plan a trip. Table 6.5 gives you a place to

Table 6.5 Planning Trip Costs

Trip Expense Item	*Estimated Cost*
Gasoline	
Tolls (road, bridge) and parking	
Hotels, motels, inns	
Campgrounds and RV (caravan) parks	
Food in restaurants	
Food cooked at campsites or eaten at picnics	
Admissions costs and parks passes	
Souvenirs	
Emergencies and other costs	
Estimated total trip cost	

start calculating your expenses. Table 6.6 is a mileage- and time-estimating tool. Figure 6.5 is a checklist so you can decide if you remembered everything you need to consider. Remember to keep your driving distances short on days you plan to tour (sightsee). And always keep in mind that everything costs more than you expect (plan), so it is better to use the more expensive (higher) costs and always round up.

6.3.7 Reassess Your Plans If Costs Exceed Your Budget

Sometimes after you do your research, you decide you can't afford the trip. Maybe you could go another time when there are fewer people traveling and pay lower off-peak, off-season rates. You might be able to find less expensive hotels or spend more time camping. You could cook more of your own meals. Or you might have to pick another place this time.

The only way you can do this is to have a plan, do your research, and estimate costs.

6.4 USING AND READING A MAP

Maps are very useful documents. They contain an amazing amount of information in a small space. In addition, the areas the maps depict (cover) are logically represented on the map. When the map covers (shows) a city,

Table 6.6 Mileage and Time Estimates

Day/Mileage/Activities	*Mileage*	*Driving Time*	*Activities Planned (Sightseeing, Driving, or Both)*
Day 1			
Day 2			
Day 3			
Day 4			
Day 5			
Day 6			
Day 7			
Day 8			
Day 9			
Day 10			

- ❑ Research trip options—online, ask friends, read books, and collect brochures.
- ❑ Plan length of trip.
- ❑ Develop basic budget.
- ❑ Estimate costs for trip: fuel, fees, hotels, campgrounds, food, admissions, souvenirs, and emergencies.
- ❑ Get maps.
- ❑ Go to automobile club or websites to get road information and trip-planning tips and assistance.
- ❑ Read maps and choose best routes.
- ❑ Contact campgrounds and hotels to make reservations and get cost information.
- ❑ Fill out table 6.5.
- ❑ Fill out table 6.6.
- ❑ Revise plans, budget, or destination if necessary.
- ❑ Pack, load the car, and enjoy your trip.

Figure 6.5 Trip-Planning Checklist

the city usually has certain logical features that make a map even more useful.

If you know a few basic (simple) things about maps and the areas they cover, you can make your life much easier. First you need to read the legend, which is the list of symbols used in the map. Then you need to know a bit about applying this information to the area the map covers. Once you know these two things, you will find getting around cities and driving across the country or to a tourist destination to be very easy.

6.4.1 Using a Map in the City

Most cities in America are organized (laid out) in very logical ways. The street names have meanings and numbers, the distance between streets is consistent (the same), and some roads are more important than others (through streets).

Cities are usually laid out on a grid (square or rectangle) system. The roads and streets form the grid. Normally, there is a set (fixed) number of streets in each grid. The number of streets (blocks) may be one amount (number) from north to south and a different number from east to west.

Knowing these grids and the distance between streets makes getting around very simple. Figure 6.6 explains the two most common city grid systems used in America.

Why is the information in figure 6.6 so useful? First, if you know how many blocks away a place is, you can count the number of blocks and figure out how far you have to walk or drive. You can get a good idea how long it will take to get somewhere. You will be able to decide which bus to take. Figure 6.7 shows you how to use the city grid to figure out (estimate) how long it should take to go somewhere.

If you use a map, you can figure out the best (fastest) route if you understand the map legend (symbols). Some roads are faster than other roads because there are more lanes or fewer traffic lights, or because access is limited (controlled). These are better (faster) roads when you are going from one place directly to another and don't need (want) to make any other stops. Sometimes the shortest, most direct route is not the fastest route. It may make sense to drive a bit farther (more) if you can avoid traffic or lights and stay on wider, faster roads.

City # 1

- Grid size: 1 mile from north to south (or south to north) and 1 mile from east to west (or west to east)
- Number of blocks from north to south (or south to north): 10
- Number of blocks from east to west (or west to east): 10
- Length on one block from north to south (or south to north): 1/10 mile
- Length of one block from east to west (or west to east): 1/10 mile

Note: This is the actual grid layout (at least from north to south or south to north) for New York City.

City # 2

- Grid size: 1/2 mile from north to south (or south to north), 1/2 mile from east to west (or west to east)
- Number of blocks from north to south (or south to north): 4
- Number of blocks from east to west (or west to east): 8
- Length on one block from north to south (or south to north): 1/8 mile
- Length of one block from east to west (or west to east): 1/16 mile

Note: This is the actual grid layout and block length for Denver, Colorado.

Figure 6.6 Grid Examples

- You are in a city built on (with) a 1-mile grid (north to south and east to west), and there are 10 blocks in 1 mile both north-south and east-west.
- You need to go the doctor's office.
- You look up the address, and find it on your map.
- You count how many blocks north (or south) you need to go.
- You then count how many blocks east (or west) you need to go.
- Then you multiply the total number of blocks you need to travel by 1/10 since each block is 1/10 mile in length.
- If you have to go 87 blocks south and 14 blocks east, you have to travel:

$$87\ 1/10 = 87/1\ 1/10 = (87\ 1) \div (1\ 10) = 87/10 = 8.7 \text{ miles}$$

- Now you can begin to estimate the amount of time (how long) it will take you to get to your appointment.
- If you are driving in the city, you will have to stop for traffic lights and slow or stopped traffic. The speed limit may be 30 mph, but your average (actual) speed will be much slower.
- If you could drive 30 mph, it would take you 2 minutes to drive one mile, so it would take you:

$$2\ 8.7 = 17.4 \text{ minutes}$$

- You will probably only average 15 mph, so it will take twice as long to get there since you are going half as fast:

$$17.4\ 2 = 34.8 \text{ minutes}$$

Figure 6.7 Calculating Distance and Time

Second, you need to know how cities assign numbers to houses, buildings, and streets. Most cities assign each block a series of numbers for addresses. Generally a block gets a series of 100 numbers for addresses (although not all numbers are used). New York City is a major exception to this numbering system.

One north-south street is assigned the numbers from 000 to 099. All other north-south blocks to the east will be numbered from this point. The next north-south street, going east, is numbered 100 to 199, the next block is 200 to 299, and so forth. The same system applies to the north-south streets on the west side of this key street. So the first street to the west is numbered 000 to 099, the next one 100 to 199, and so forth. The first eastbound street is also numbered 000 to 099, the next eastbound street on the north is numbered 100 to 199, and so forth. The same applies to the first and subsequent (next) streets on the south.

Each street has both a name and a number. It usually also has a direction (north, south, east, or west). The number normally ends in "00" and is taken from the lowest numbered building on the street. North-south streets with numbers 000 to 099 will be numbered 000; so will east-west streets numbered 000 to 099. The streets with numbers 100 to 199 will be numbered 100, and the streets with numbers 200 to 299 will be numbered 200. Since there are four streets with the number 100 (or 200, or 300, or 1200, etc.) we need to be able to tell them apart. (Note: There are four because there are two east-west streets with the number 100, and two north-south streets with the number 100. There are two east-west streets with the number 200, and two north-south streets with the number 200, and so forth.)

Most cities solve this problem as follows. East-west streets can include a "north" or "south" to let people know which way to go. North-south streets can include an "east" or "west." In addition, street names often follow a pattern such as related names, numbers, or other pattern so you know which side of the "000" line to find them. How does this numbering system help you find your way around? Let's look at a street address (figure 6.8) and find out.

The best way to really understand this explanation is to go out in your own city or town and walk around. Look for the numbers on the street signs. As you walk from one block to the next, you will see the numbers change. If you are walking toward one of the "000" streets, you will see the block numbers on the street signs go down (decline). If you are walking away, you will see the numbers go up (increase).

6.4.2 Practice Exercises

a. Take a walk around the downtown area of your city or town. Find out where the two "000" streets are. Then walk along one of the streets and note what happens to the street numbers. Write down what you observe (see).

b. Find out how many blocks are in your city or town grid. Find out how many blocks are in 1 mile going north-south and in 1 mile going east-

- You need to go to 427 East Smith Avenue for a party.
- Since the address is "east," you know Smith Avenue is an east-west street.
- You also know you are looking for the block with the numbers 400 to 499 since 427 is between 400 and 499.
- Since the numbers are 400 to 499, the block will be numbered 400.
- You don't know how far north or south of the other "000" number (the east-west "000" line) Smith Avenue is.
- You can use a map to find Smith Avenue and then find the two "000" streets.
- An easier way is to ask what the cross street is (the nearest north-south street) and what its number is. Then you can find the two "000" streets (north-south and east-west), and you will be able to find Smith Avenue and the cross street very easily.
- If the cross street is North Jones Road, and its number is 1100, you know the following:
- You need to go 11 blocks north of the point where the two "000" numbered blocks cross (intersect).
- That will bring you to Smith Avenue.
- You need to go four blocks east on Smith Avenue. That will bring you to the 400 block.
- You need to go along the 400 block of Smith Avenue and look for #427.

Figure 6.8 Sample Street Address

west. Walk 1/2 mile and see how long it takes you. (This is also a great way to see how long you should allow when you have to walk somewhere.)

c. Estimate the number of blocks from your home to a place you go often, such as a grocery store. Figure out how many miles those blocks equal. Estimate how long you expect it to take to walk or drive there. Was your estimate accurate?

If you look at the city map, you will see some useful information in the legend. A legend is a code section that explains the symbols used on the map. It shows types of roads: highways, two-lane streets, four-lane streets, limited access (fast) roads, and other roads. The legend also has codes for buildings, churches, greenbelts and parks, radio towers, rivers, lakes, and much more. If you are trying to find the state capitol building, you can find the street on the map and find the symbol in the legend to get the exact location. Legends are somewhat different on different maps. Always consult (look at) the legend when you first use a map or need to find some place.

One more key item you will always find in a legend: a bar that shows distance. Normally the legend will indicate 1″ = X, where X is the number of feet or miles that bar equates to (equals or shows).

6.4.3 Using a Map on the Highway

You can get excellent highway maps from an automobile club, tourist information agency (office), gasoline service station, bookstore, or online map service, to name a few places. Make sure your map is no more than one year old, since new roads are always being built. You can also buy an atlas, a collection of maps for the entire country or world, at many bookstores and other stores. Take time to look over (study) the maps you will need for your trip. Read the legend and find its symbols (roads, exits, buildings, tourist sights, rivers, lakes, bridges, campgrounds, and so forth) on your map.

The scale of the map tells (shows) you how many miles are in one inch (1″). It may also tell you how many kilometers are in 1 inch, but that isn't going to help much on your trip in America. Few road information signs in the United States show metric measurements. You can take a ruler (straight edge) that is marked in inches and lay it along your route to estimate the distance you need to drive. Roads curve and rulers don't, so this is only a rough (not very close) estimate (approximation).

Look at the route you plan to follow. The map legend will show you how highway exits (on and off ramps) are marked. These exits are almost always numbered, and they may sometimes include letters. Exit signs along the highway will use these exit numbers. The exits are numbered in one of two ways: Either they are in sequence (111, 112, 113, etc.) or they are in an order that corresponds to the number of miles from a state's border (edge).

When exits are numbered in sequence, there is no relation to the actual number of miles between each exit. This approach (numbering system) is used in more crowded parts of America. If there are multiple (many, several) exits in a very short distance, it isn't possible to use numbers that correspond with (match) the number of miles from the state border (line, edge).

When exit numbers correspond with (match) the number of miles from the edge (border) of a state, you know that it is 24 miles between exit 234 and exit 258. All you need to do is subtract the smaller number from the larger one. (See sidebar 6.1.)

Maps have another very useful feature for long-distance driving. In addition to the legend telling (showing) you exit numbers, there are little (tiny) triangles above each exit. If you look along the highway to the next exit, you will see another tiny triangle in the same color. Somewhere in between the two triangles will be a small number in the same color as the triangles. This number is the number of miles (distance, mileage) between the two exits. This is particularly helpful when the highway exits are numbered in order (sequence) rather than corresponding to actual miles from one edge of the state.

Note that exit numbering and the little highway mileage signs start over when you enter a new state. Also, mileage is measured from one edge of the state, beginning with 0, so if you begin at the other edge (border) the numbers will start at a high point and decrease to 0 at the other edge.

Mileage Markers on Highways

As you drive along many state, U.S., and interstate highways, look to the side or center of the road. You will begin to notice small signs with a number on them. These signs are usually green and white and measure about 4″ by 6″. The numbers are actually mileage measurements. These measurements tell you the distance to one edge of the state (north or south; east or west). In states where highway exits use mileage measurements as their numbers, these small mileage signs can be very useful. If you need to take exit 46, and you just passed mileage sign 45, *and* the mileage signs are increasing in value, you are almost at your exit. You have less than one mile to drive. If the mileage signs are decreasing in value, you either missed your exit or are looking for the wrong exit number.

Sidebar 6.1

6.4.4 Using a Map in the National Parks and Other Tourist Attractions

Tourist attractions such as Disneyland, national parks, state parks, battlefields, historic sites, and other places almost always have their own maps. You usually get these maps for free when you pay the fee to enter the attraction.

These maps are very useful, but unless they are drawn (designed) by a government or professional map-making service, they may not be very accurate (standardized). Attractions such as Sea World or Disneyland do not use (follow) standard legends. However, state and national parks and many historic sites have maps that are standardized, so they are more accurate. In addition to normal legend information, you will see symbols (codes) for each major sight (geysers, battle sites, historic buildings, and so forth). The maps may also give you an approximate idea of how long it takes to get to a sight, or how long it takes to see the sight.

6.4.5 Using a Map to Get around Locally

One of the best ways to learn your way around a new city or town is to get a local map and study it. Once you are familiar with the legend and the main streets, you can use the map in many ways. Take it with you when you walk or drive around.

There are several good places to get free or low-cost (in expensive) maps of your city and state. Tourist information offices have maps, and these maps are almost always free. All you have (need) to do is go to their office and ask. You don't have to be a tourist to get maps. Chambers of commerce often (usually) sell maps of their city and state. Automobile clubs have maps for their members, and these maps are usually free. Finally, you can download maps from a website such as Mapquest (www.mapquest.com). These maps can include very detailed (specific) directions for driving to places. Even better, you can get directions that give (show, tell) you the fastest route, or directions that give (show, tell) you the shortest route. Remember, though, that the shortest route may not be the fastest route!

All maps include a legend. Legends are usually in one corner of the map. Maps may be two-sided (printed on both sides), and the legend may only be on one side. The legend will give you the scale of the map. The scale is a model that shows you how many miles are in one inch. Figure 6.9 shows you some things you can learn from a legend.

When you are learning your way around a city, it is helpful to know the length and width of a normal (typical) block. Then you can plan how long it should take to walk or drive somewhere. You can measure the length of a block by using your car's odometer. To find the length of a block, drive the length of four or five blocks, then divide your mileage reading by the number of blocks you just drove. This is more accurate (precise) than only driving one block. Repeat the process (steps) to measure the width. Again you should drive the width of four or five blocks, not just one. Figure 6.10 shows (tells) you exactly how to do this calculation.

There are two more ways to measure the length and width of a block:

1. See how many minutes it takes you to walk one block along its length (north-south) and again along its width (east-west). Most people take about 20 minutes to walk one mile. If you are a fast walker, you might take 17–19 minutes to walk one mile. If you are a slow walker, it might take you 21–23 minutes. Divide the amount of time it takes you to walk one block by the amount of time you think it takes you to walk one mile. The answer will be a decimal that is the portion of a mile you just walked. So the width (or length) of a block is that many miles. Your answer will be significantly less than one. If you need 20 minutes to walk one mile, and it takes you 2.5 minutes (two minutes and 30 seconds) to walk the length of one block, here is the calculation for the length of one block: 2.5 minutes

Scale: number of miles in 1″	Distance between cities
Road type—U.S. highway, state, city, interstate	Rivers and streams
Churches	Campgrounds
Points of interest	Mountains
Scenic routes	Deserts
Exits and their numbers	Bridges and tunnels
Distance between exits	Toll roads, bridges, and tunnels
	Parks

Figure 6.9 Information in a Map Legend

To calculate the length of a block:

- Note the mileage on the odometer (the place that shows the number of miles you have driven). You need to note the entire number, including tenths of a mile. If you have a "trip meter" (a special odometer you can reset to zero to measure how far you are driving), reset it to 0.
- Drive your car along several blocks in a north or south direction.
- Stop, and note your odometer or trip meter reading (measurement).
- Divide this number by the number of blocks you just drove.
- The result is the length of a block going north-south.

To calculate the width of a block:

- Note the mileage on the odometer (the place that shows the number of miles you have driven). You need to note the entire number, including tenths of a mile. If you have a "trip meter" (a special odometer you can reset to zero to measure how far you are driving), reset it to 0.
- Drive your car along several blocks in an east or west direction.
- Stop, and note your odometer or trip meter reading (measurement).
- Divide this number by the number of blocks you just drove.
- The result is the width of a block going east-west.
- In some cities, blocks are longer in one direction than the other. In other cities, the length and width of a block are about the same.
- If you are in a suburb with winding (curving, irregular) streets, this process will not work.

Figure 6.10 Calculating the Length and Width of a Block

÷ 20 minutes/mile = 0.125 miles per block. That is the same as 1/8 mile, so there are eight blocks per mile (north-south). Repeat the process for the other (east-west) direction.

2. Measure your pace (the length of your step or stride) and then walk the length and width of a block. If your pace (stride) is 2.5 feet (which is about average) and you walk about 210 steps, you have walked 2.5 feet/step · 210 steps = 525 feet. Since there are 5,280 feet in one mile, you have walked about 1/10 mile (525 ÷ 5,280 = 0.1). So there are 10 blocks in 1 mile. Then you need to repeat the process for the other direction.

6.5 PAYING TAXES

No one gets very excited at the thought of paying taxes. Still, it is part of life in America and almost everywhere else. For most people, taxes are hard to avoid. Sales tax (MOM, VAT, GST) is added to most purchases. Federal, state, local, city, and Social Security taxes are taken out of your gross pay before you get your check. Some taxes, such as property taxes, you may pay yourself. However, most people pay those taxes as part of their mortgage payment.

If you are self-employed or own a business, you will have to take out (withhold) many different types of taxes from your pay and from your employees' pay. You will have to make sure the money you withhold (take out) is sent to the right (correct) place at the proper (right, scheduled) time. If you own a business, you probably will collect sales tax, and you have to send that money to the right places at the right time, too. In America, there are very steep (severe, heavy) fines and penalties if you do not pay the full amount of taxes on time.

Most states have sales tax on most of the things you buy. Generally, this tax ranges from 3 to 10%. It is not normally applied to services, just to goods (merchandise). You need to calculate this amount when you are estimating the cost of things you are buying. Sales tax is not usually included in the price marked on an item.

Most states have a state income tax. This amount ranges from 1 to 10% of your income. Some cities also have an income tax of 2 to 8%. These taxes are withheld from your gross pay (earnings) if you are an employee. If you are a business owner (employer), you are responsible for withholding this money from your pay and the pay of your employees. You must send the money to the state and/or city on time or pay fines, penalties, and interest.

The federal government has an income tax. The amount you pay varies based on your income. You can reduce your taxable income in several ways. If you have a mortgage, pay property tax, pay state/city tax, or donate items to charity, you may be able to reduce the amount of income you pay federal income tax on. If you contribute to some retirement plans, you may also be able to reduce the amount of federal tax you pay. Federal tax is based on "brackets." The best way to see what brackets apply to you is to talk with a tax advisor or go to the Internal Revenue Service (IRS) website at www.irs.gov.

You must also pay Social Security tax, including Medicare tax. The Social Security portion ends at some point (about $90,000 in income per person), but the Medicare portion does not end. The Medicare portion is about 1.45% of your total income; the Social Security portion is about 6.2% of a certain amount of your income. If you are an employer, you must contribute the same amounts for each employee.

6.5.1 Practice Exercise

a. Take out a pay stub (a listing of your earnings and taxes) and calculate what percent of your gross income is paid for:

- Social Security tax
- Medicare tax
- State tax
- City tax
- Federal tax
- Health insurance
- Retirement savings

If you don't understand the entries on your earnings statement, go to your human resources department and ask for someone to explain the numbers to you.

6.6 SAVING AND INVESTING

In America, you have to plan for your own retirement. You also have to save money for the things you want to buy and the trips you want to take. You usually have to pay for your children's education, too.

You have many choices for saving and investing your money:

- Company retirement plans
- Individual retirement accounts (IRAs)
- Personal savings—bank accounts, mutual funds, stocks, bonds, certificates of deposit (CDs), and the like

- Your home—as it grows in value
- Rental property
- Your business
- College savings plans

No matter how you decide to accumulate money, the most important thing is to do it! Regular savings and investing are critical to your future in America.

When you invest (save) money, you get "interest," "dividends" (on bonds), or a "rate of return." This is what makes (allows, causes) your money (assets) to grow (increase in value). There is another aspect to consider, too—compounding.

6.6.1 Compounding

Compounding is the most important part of growing your money. When you earn (get) 5% for your savings and investments, and you reinvest (don't take out) that money, you will have even more money over time (in the future). Table 6.7 compares "simple" interest and interest that "compounds"—where you earn "interest on your interest."

Obviously there is real value (importance) to compounding your money (investments)! If you projected (extended) the results in table 6.7 below, you could estimate the value of your money in 24 years, 36 years, and so forth. The way you do this is by using the Rule of 72, shown in figure 6.11.

The longer you can let your money grow (compound), the more money you will have later—at retirement, to pay for college, to buy a new car, to make a down payment on a house. If you can earn a higher rate of return, your money will increase (grow, compound) even more quickly. If you can add to your savings (investments) each month, week, or year, you will have even more money.

6.6.2 Practice Exercises

a. What rate of return (such as an interest rate or dividend rate) do you need to earn to double your money in 10 years? Assume that all earnings

Table 6.7 Simple versus Compound Interest

Simple Interest	Compound Interest
If you earn 6% per year, and you start with $10,000, you will earn $600 every year. If you take the money (earnings, interest) and spend it each year, you will still have $10,000. If you keep the $600, but do not earn interest on it, at the end of 12 years you would have your original $10,000, plus $600/year · 12 years = $7,200. So you would have $10,000 plus $7,200, or $17,200.	If you earn 6% per year, and you start with $10,000, you will earn $600 every year. If you take the money (earnings, interest) and spend it each year, you will still have $10,000. If you reinvest the $600 each year and earn interest on it, you are *compounding* your original money. You will have more money than someone who spends the $600 each year, or someone who does not earn interest on the $600 each year. In fact, you will have about $20,000 at the end of 12 years.
Year 1: $600 + $10,000 = $10,600	Year 1: $10,000 + $600 = $10,600
Year 2: $600 + $10,600 = $11,200	Year 2: $10,600 + $636 = $11,236
Year 3: $600 + $11,200 = $11,800	Year 3: $11,236 + $674 = $11,910
Year 4: $600 + $11,800 = $12,400	Year 4: $11,910 + $715 = $12,625
Year 5: $600 + $12,400 = $13,000	Year 5: $12,625 + $758 = $13,383
Year 6: $600 + $13,000 = $13,600	Year 6: $13,383 + $803 = $14,186
Year 7: $600 + $13,600 = $14,200	Year 7: $14,186 + $851 = $15,037
Year 8: $600 + $14,200 = $14,800	Year 8: $15,037 + $902 = $15,939
Year 9: $600 + $14,800 = $15,400	Year 9: $15,939 + $956 = $16,895
Year 10: $600 + $15,400 = $16,000	Year 10: $16,895 + $1,014 = $17,909
Year 11: $600 + $16,000 = $16,600	Year 11: $17.909 + $1,075 = $18,984
Year 12: $600 + $16,600 = $17,200	Year 12: $18,984 + $1,139 = $20,123

Money "compounds" or grows faster if you reinvest dividends, interest, or other earnings. This increases the principal (original) amount you began with at the fastest possible rate. You earn "interest on interest." Here is a quick way to figure out (calculate) how fast your money will grow:

Divide the interest rate into 72. The answer is the number of years it will take to double your money. So, if you earn 6% on your mutual funds and earn that same rate (amount) every year, it will take you 12 years to double your original money.

If you started with $10,000, and earn 6% per year, you should have $20,000 after 12 years. Of course you must reinvest all the money to get the result shown here. You must also keep earning at least 6%.

Figure 6.11 The Rule of 72

(interest) are reinvested, not taken out (spent, used). If you could earn 15%, how long would it take to double your money?
b. Which is better: Earning 6% per year for 10 years (with no compounding—just simple interest) or earning 5% per year (with compounding) for 14 years?

Answers:

a. About 7%; about 5 years. Use the Rule of 72.
b. You will have a bit more money earning 5% (compounded) than 6% (simple interest).

6.6.3 Compounding and Buying a Home or Rental Property

Other investments also benefit from compounding—the Rule of 72 still applies. For example, if you buy a house or rental unit (property) for $200,000 and put $20,000 "down" (as a down payment), your house or property should grow in value. Your investment will increase in two ways. First, the value of the house (property) itself should increase. Second, if you look at the increase in the value of your property against (versus) the amount of money you invested, you may get (have, enjoy) a very large rate of return.
Here's why. If you paid $200,000 for a home (house, property) and the value increases by 4% per year, your value at the end of 18 years will be about $400,000 (72 ÷ 4% = 18 years). Remember that you invested (made a down payment of) $20,000. This means that you have a mortgage for $180,000. You have only used (tied up, committed) $20,000 of your own money. If the house goes up in value by 4%, the increase in value the first year is 4% · $200,000 = 0.04 · $200,000 = $8,000. Since you only invested $20,000 of your own (personal) money, your rate of return (interest rate) is about 40% the first year. This is why people buy houses and take out (use) mortgages for most (much) of the cost. They do not have to commit (put in) a lot of their own money, yet they get the benefit of any rise (increase) in the home's value.

6.6.4 Practice Exercise

a. You are going to buy a $150,000 rental property (building, house, apartment) and put $25,000 as a down payment. You expect the property to increase in value by 6% per year. How much should your rental property grow (increase) in value the first year? How many years would it take to double the value of your property if it continues to increase (compound) at 6% per year? About how much would the rental property be worth after 12 years? After 24 years? What is the rate of return on your investment ($25,000) the first year?

Answer:

a. 6% · $150,000 = $9,000; 12 years; $300,000; $600,000; about 36%.

6.6.5 Saving for Retirement, College, or Other Reasons

In America, you do not receive much help from the government (federal, state, or local) when you are planning to retire. Social Security is a program that is intended to supplement (support, increase) the money you saved for your retirement. Social Security was never intended to be someone's entire pension, or source of retirement income. This is very different from most other countries in the world.

In order to have a comfortable (enjoyable) retirement, you need to have other sources of income. Many employers will help you accumulate (save) money for retirement, but they may not simply give you money. You need to understand the savings options you have available through your employer and the options (choices) you have for personal savings and investments.

In order to encourage people to save money for retirement and other needs, the federal and state governments provide incentives (encouragement) to both employees and employers.

As an employee, you may be able to put money in certain retirement plans without paying taxes. In most cases, these taxes are *deferred*—they will be due (payable) some day, but not today. In fact, these taxes are normally not due until you retire, or until you take the money out and use it. There are a number of retirement plans that fall into this "tax-deferred" category:

- 401(k) plans
- 403(b) plans
- Individual retirement accounts (IRAs):
  - Simple IRAs
  - Deductible IRAs
  - Nondeductible IRAs
  - Roth IRAs (these are not tax-deferred, but the increase in value is not taxed at retirement, either)
- Profit-sharing plans (PSPs)

As an employer, the government provides incentives to encourage you to help your employees save for retirement. You are able to give (match) a portion of the money your employees contribute to (save in) certain retirement plans. The most common plans that allow (encourage) matching by the employer are:

- 401(k) plans
- 403(b) plans
- Simple individual retirement accounts
- Profit-sharing plans

There are other retirement plans available, but these are the ones you are most likely to see (encounter, have available).

Why should you be interested in retirement savings plans that only defer taxes? If you will have to pay taxes one day anyway, why not pay them today and be done with it?

There are several reasons. First, most people are not very good savers. Avoiding paying taxes is a good incentive (encouragement) for them to do something that will be very valuable in a few years. Second, many people will owe taxes at a lower rate when they retire. They will be in a lower *tax bracket*. This means they will pay less in taxes in the future than they would pay today. Third, there is the value of compounding. If you invest more money because you didn't have to pay taxes first, you will have more money when you do pay taxes at retirement.

Finally, in many retirement plans your employer will match part or all of the money you contribute (put in). That means if you put in 3% of your salary, your employer will *give* you the same amount. That is free money!

Contributing to a Retirement Plan	Not Contributing to a Retirement Plan
Salary = $3,000/month	
Contribution % = 4% = $120	Salary = $3,000 per month
Employer match = 4% = $120	Federal, state, local taxes = 25%
Federal, state, local taxes = 25%	Social Security taxes = 7.65%
Tax savings = 25% · $120 = $30	Take-home pay = $2,020.50
Social Security taxes = 7.65%	
Take home pay = $2020.50 − $90 = $1,930.50	
Rate of return = 8%	
Take-home pay is $90 less.	Take-home pay is $90 more.
Taxes are $30 less.	Taxes are $30 more.
Monthly retirement savings $150 with employer match.	No monthly retirement savings.
	No retirement savings.
Estimated annual return on retirement savings is 8%.	None.
	None.
Amount of employee contribution for 30 years: $27,000.	
Value of retirement savings after 30 years: almost $225,000	

Figure 6.12 Weighing the Pros and Cons: Retirement Contributions

Here is another way to look at it: If you put 3% of your gross pay into a retirement account, and you are earning $2,500 per month, you are putting $75 into your retirement plan. If your employer is matching that contribution, you are getting another $75 per month. You are also earning a rate of return on both your contribution and your employer's contribution. Your employer's contribution is 100% of your contribution, so you are "earning" 100% on your $75. On top of (in addition to) that, if you earn 6% per year on your money and your employer's contribution, you are getting even more money!

You will have less money to spend because you are contributing to your retirement account, but not $75 less because you are not paying federal, state, or local taxes (just Social Security and Medicare taxes). Take a look at figure 6.12 to get an idea of the benefits and costs of contributing to retirement plan when your employer matches your contribution.

With this strategy, free money from your employer match, a reasonable rate of return (8%), a planned (disciplined) savings approach, and 30 years of working really pay off.

6.7 CONVERTING A RECIPE

You probably didn't bring your cooking supplies (pots, pans, measuring spoons, scales, and cookbooks) with you from your home country. Now you need to buy new baking, cooking, and measuring tools (utensils). They will use ASM, not metric, amounts. In order to cook your favorite foods, you will need to convert their measurements from metric to ASM. You also need to convert the cooking temperatures to °F.

Cooking times should not be affected unless you are living at an elevation above 3,500 feet (about 1,000 meters).

Let's start with the easy conversion—the temperature. If you are going to bake a cake, you need to preheat (warm up) the oven before you start. If your cake recipe calls for (reads) "Bake at 175°C for 1 hour," what is the temperature in Fahrenheit? Go back to chapter 1 (to the section on conversions) if you need help (assistance). Figure 6.13 shows you how to do the temperature conversion.

Now let's look at the actual ingredients for your recipe. Remember that the conversions are close (approximate) but not exact. If most of the metric measurements convert to ASM amounts that are "a bit less than" or "nearly the same," you need to be careful with any metric measurements that convert to ASM amounts that are "a bit more than." If the differences are too great (big), your recipe won't come out right (won't work). The same is true if most of the conversions are "a bit more than" and one or two are "a bit less than." You may have to try several adjustments (variations) to get your home recipes to convert to ASM. The results will be

To convert 175°C to Fahrenheit:

- Multiply 175 by 9/5 = 315.
- Add 32 to the result: 315 + 32 = 347°F, or about 350°F.

Figure 6.13 Cooking Temperature Conversion

worth the effort (worthwhile)! Figure 6.14 shows a recipe that has been converted to and from metric and ASM.

The amounts in figure 6.14 were easy to convert. All the conversions were "a bit less than," so you shouldn't need to make any other adjustments. Note that you don't make any changes to ingredients with a (non-metric) unit value, so eggs and bananas stay the same for either ASM or metric. You would only change unit measures if the overall recipe changed significantly (proportionately) during the conversion process.

If you needed 13 ml of vanilla extract rather than 10 ml or 15 ml, that is a significant difference. Ten ml is 22% less than 13 ml, so it will affect the entire recipe. Thirteen ml is also about 13% less than 15 ml, so that will also affect your recipe's proportions. If all your other measures are "a bit less than" when they are converted (for example, 1 cup is a bit less than 250 ml), you should round the vanilla extract amount down to 10 ml (or 2 tsp) rather than up to 15 ml (or 3 tsp or 1 tbs). You may still need to add a bit more vanilla extract to make things taste right if you round down. Take a look at the rounding tip in sidebar 6.2 if you need some help with deciding whether to round up or down.

Many times, your recipe calls for (needs) ingredients (items) not sold in local stores. You may find specialty markets (shops) selling what you need. If not, you can usually find acceptable (workable) substitutes you can buy in local stores. These substitutes may affect your recipes, though. For example, they may change the proportions (amounts) of other items. You will have to try and see what works best.

Metric	**ASM**
Preheat your oven to 175°C.	Preheat your oven to 350°F.
Assemble (collect) the following ingredients:	Assemble (collect) the following ingredients:
2 eggs	2 eggs
10 ml vanilla extract	2 tsp vanilla extract
5 ml salt	1 tsp salt
10 ml baking powder	2 tsp baking powder
250 ml brown sugar	1 c. brown sugar
500 ml flour	2 c. flour
3 bananas	3 bananas

Figure 6.14 Banana Bread Recipe Conversion

Rounding Tip

Always try to round measurements either all up or all down. You will not need to make as many adjustments that way.

Sidebar 6.2

6.7.1 Practice Exercise

Convert one of your favorite recipes from metric to ASM. Then make a shopping list using ASM so you can buy the right amounts. Don't forget to convert the cooking temperature if necessary. Use figure 6.15 to list the information.

6.8 USING A COMPASS

America is a big place. We have lots of wide, wild, open spaces. It's easy to get lost in a national or state forest or park, or to take a wrong turn in a ski area. One way to help yourself is to have, and know how to use, a compass. In section 6.8.1, you'll learn some very basic tips on using a compass to reduce your chances of getting lost. Of course, if you hike or ski in the backcountry (forests and parks) often, you should take a good wilderness skills course. Either way, *never* go to these areas alone, and

Metric Amounts	ASM Amounts
Shopping List in ASM	

Figure 6.15 Recipe Conversion

always tell someone where you're going and when you plan to return. Cell phones may not work in the wilderness (backcountry).

Have you been hiking or camping yet? Surrounded by trees, it's beautiful, but it's also hard to see where you're going. Even on a marked path you can get lost. You might choose the wrong path, or you might be on a game (animal, deer) trail instead of a real path. Even with a map, you can get lost.

Have you been skiing or snowboarding yet? It seems like it should be hard to get lost in a big open snowfield, doesn't it? Actually, with the trees along the sides and the snow everywhere (including falling from the sky!) it's quite easy to get lost.

6.8.1 Using a Compass to Find Your Way

How can a compass help? First, you need to understand how a compass works. Figure 6.16 is a simple picture of a compass showing north (0°), northeast (45°), east (90°), southeast (135°), south (180°), southwest (225°), west (270°), and northwest (315°).

A compass is divided into 360 units called "degrees." The symbol for degrees on a compass is a ° just as for temperature, but the ° symbol is not followed by a C (for centigrade) or F (for Fahrenheit). Degrees around a circle or compass are absolute units whether you are working with metric or ASM. You do not have to do any conversions.

Let's start with a simple circle as shown in figure 6.16. Then we'll look at how this equates to (compares to) a compass. The numbers around a circle are standard. Zero (0°) is always at the top. It is the "degree" equivalent of north. Its opposite, 180°, is always at the bottom. This is the "degree" equivalent of south. So 90° is always to the right of the circle and

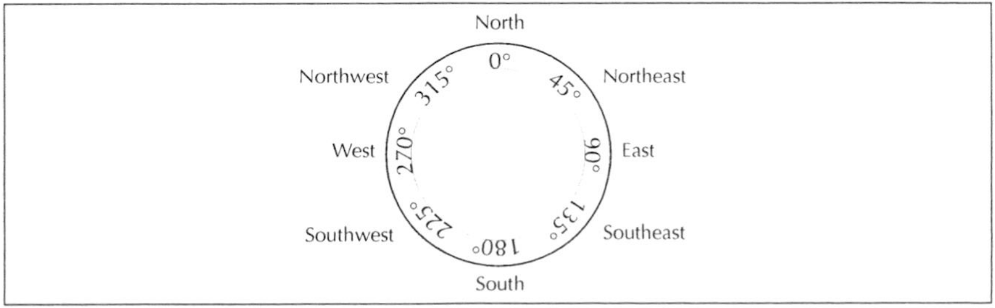

Figure 6.16 The Compass

represents east. That leaves 270°, or west, which is always to the left of the circle. In between these measurements, you have a few other standard equivalents: 45° is equivalent to northeast, 135° is equivalent to southeast, 225° is equivalent to southwest, and 315° is equivalent to northwest.

Since you can rotate (turn, orient) a compass any direction, the needle is "magnetized." This means it is coated (painted) with a material that is attracted to the North Pole, so the compass needle will always point north (or close enough to north to be useful to you). This is equivalent to the circle on the previous page. Once you know north is considered to be "up," you can determine east (90°), south (180°), and west (270°) by looking at your compass.

How does this help you understand (figure out) where you are going (heading)? As long as you know the compass always points (indicates, shows) north, you can decide what direction you are going or need to go. If you were facing north, the compass needle should align itself with the 0° line. If you allow the needle to align with (point to, line up with) the 90° mark and you walk that direction, you are not walking north. Think about it. If you now turn 90° to your left, you are facing west. The compass needle still points north, but it is aligned with the 90° line. You have turned "90° west of north." As long as you keep the compass needle to your right, and you travel in a fairly (relatively) straight line, you will be walking west.

This is not intuitively (immediately, truly, really) obvious. You need to practice with a compass, starting out facing north, and then turn to the different points shown on the circle in figure 6.16. Then see which degree line your compass needle is aligned with when you are looking along the zero (0°) degree line.

In order to return the way you came, you need to know the direction you are currently walking. Then you have to head in the complete opposite direction. The complete opposite direction means turning 180° so you are going the other way. To get the opposite, add 180° to the heading (number in degrees) the north-pointing needle is aligned with. Then align the north-pointing needle over this new heading. You will see you have to turn the other way to do this. If the result when you add 180 to the current heading is 360 or greater, you need to subtract 360 from your answer (since a compass only goes to 360°!).

Another way to do the same thing—find your direction—is to always keep the north-pointing arrow aligned with the 0° or north heading. When you choose your direction of travel, you need to look along the line to that degree marker, then find a landmark (tree, building, hill, telephone pole, etc.) along that line. Head toward the landmark. When you get there, you need to find another landmark along the direction you want to go. If there are no landmarks (as in the case of a field of snow), send your partner in the direction you want to go, but no farther than you can see. Then walk to him or her. Once you are there, make sure your compass arrow is aligned north, pick a new landmark (or use your friend again), and repeat.

These approaches only work if you know where you started from (began). Always write down the direction you want to travel in relation to your starting point. You may start from your car (for a hike), a ski lift, or other point. Then note the heading that is 180° opposite so you can find your way back.

If you are going one direction for a while (some time) and then in another direction (heading), you need to know how far or how long you went in the first direction. If you know both the time and distance you have traveled, even better. Write this information down. You need the opposite heading to get back. Keep this information for each direction change. It's a very good idea to only change directions at (or near) landmarks. Don't forget to write down the landmarks, too.

If you are going to ski in the "back bowls" of a ski resort (area), you can get lost easily (quickly). To make getting lost less likely, apply the compass headings, time, distance, and landmark information. Don't forget to allow extra time if you have to return uphill! If it took you 10 minutes to ski to a landmark down a hill, it may take 30 minutes to get back.

How does this work? You have just ridden the ski lift to the beginning of some great open bowls. There are almost no trees in view (sight). As soon as you get off the chair lift, you and your friend decide to head to your right. So you take out your compass and align the north-pointing needle with the 0° line. You decide to go in a direction that appears to be along the 45° line when the needle is lying across the 0° line. This means you are heading northeast. You see a tree about 2 miles away, and it's right along the 45° line. You look at your watch and it's 9:30 a.m. You make a note that you are heading off at 45° and it should be about 2 miles before you stop. You also write the time down.

You reach the tree, and you see a small hill in the distance ahead of you. Before you do anything, note your arrival time at the tree. Let's say that it's 10:00 a.m. If you traveled mostly downhill, make sure you note that, too. Now write down the opposite heading (sometimes called a "back azimuth" or direction) so you can find your way back. Determine the heading to the next landmark (the small hill), and repeat the entire process. It sounds tedious (time-consuming), but it only takes a few minutes.

6.8.2 Practice Exercise

a. You and a friend are going hiking in a national forest. You plan to stay on trails most of the time, but you also want to cut across the meadows so you can save time and see the wildflowers. You have your trusty (reliable) compass and a notebook, of course. When you leave the car, there is a big open meadow, so you decide to cut across it. Before you go, what should you write down?

Heading ____________
Opposite heading ____________
Distance ____________
Time (start/end) ____________ / ____________
Landmark ________________________

You reach the far side of the meadow. You need to add a piece of information to your list above—whether the meadow was uphill, downhill, hilly, or level.

Pick your next landmark, and continue. You decide to head for a waterfall you can see in the distance. It's uphill, and you estimate it to be 4 miles away. What information should you record? (You may not need all the blank lines.)

________________________ ________________________
________________________ ________________________
________________________ ________________________
________________________ ________________________

6.8.3 Headings and Compasses on the Airplane

Aviation also depends on the use of "azimuths"—headings or directions based on a compass. If you have ever listened to a pilot talking on the radio, you have heard some things like "change to header 282" or "land on runway 47R."

In this section you'll learn a bit more about what these strange words mean. Since there are no roads in the sky, and since landmarks can be covered (hidden, obscured) by fog, snow, clouds, and so forth, pilots have to rely on the compass. They need clear directional (heading) information that is not dependent on good visibility or landmarks. That's the role of the compass.

Ground controllers give pilots directions in terms of headings. Headings are just another term for the degrees on a compass. So telling someone to follow a heading of 90 is the same as saying "go east" or "follow the 90° line." Since the pilot and ground controller know how fast the plane is traveling, it is easy to calculate how far a pilot needs to go before changing directions. Figure 6.17 is an example using headings (direction) and speed to determine how far you have flown.

The combination of heading (azimuth), speed, and time is what allows (enables) air traffic controllers to keep thousands of planes in the air without accidents. They also keep the planes at difference altitudes (heights) and keep them a certain distance apart from wing to wing, too.

When it's time for a plane to land, the pilot needs to know where to land. In many cases there are no landmarks visible until the plane is almost on the ground, so the pilot has to rely on the compass again. As a result, airport runways are given numbers that correspond to headings on the compass. If a pilot is told to land to the right on runway 45L, that means something. In fact, it means that the runway goes northeast and

- A plane is traveling 500 mph.
- The pilot is told to follow a heading of 115° for 2 hours.
- What approximate direction is the plane heading?
- How far will the plane travel in the next two hours?

Answers:

- The plane is heading between east (90°) and southeast (135°).
- Since it is going 500 mph, it will travel 1,000 miles in two hours.

Figure 6.17 Using Headings and Speed to Determine Distance

southwest since 45° is northeast, and the runway has to go the other way (225°) too! If there are parallel runways (runways going the same direction, but separated by a few hundred feet), they are usually called R (right) and L (left).

Now you may have a better idea (understanding) what you are hearing if you listen to the airplane communications during your next flight.

6.8.4 Practice Exercise

a. You are planning to get your private pilot's license. One of the questions on your exam is about headings, speed, distance, and time.

Here's the question:

You are told to fly leg #1 on a heading of 135 for one hour. You are to maintain (keep) your speed at 193 mph. Once you have flown for one hour, you are to turn to a heading of 270 (leg #2) for one and one half (1.5) hours, at a speed of 210 mph.
What direction are you flying in the first leg? ______________
How far will you fly in the second leg? ______________
What is the total distance you will fly during this trip? ______________

Answers:

You start out on a heading of southeast. You fly 193 miles, then turn to a heading of west and fly 315 more miles. You therefore are going to fly 193 + 315 = 508 miles.

b. If you are going to follow a heading of 305°, where does that fall on the compass below? Mark all the main headings (north, south, east, west, northeast, southeast, northwest, and southwest) on the drawing on page 179. Make sure to include the actual degrees, too (e.g., north = 0°).

6.9 DATES, TIMES, AND ADDRESSES

America does not generally use the 24-hour clock. The only exceptions are the military forces and some other government agencies. This means

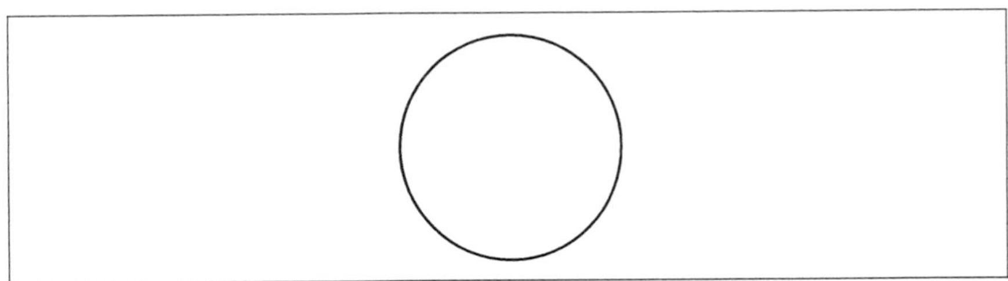

that you will have to understand the uses of "a.m." and "p.m.," since they are what differentiate (tell apart) times in the morning from times at night.

The United States also does not generally use the YYYY/MM/DD or DD/MM/YYYY form of dates. One of the few exceptions here is the customs and immigration forms. As a result, most Americans mess up those forms! We also put house or apartment numbers and zip codes in odd places. Finally, you are very likely to see Roman numerals used, especially on some clocks and at the end of movies to indicate the year in which the movie was produced.

6.9.1 The Clocks

If you misunderstand a time, you may go to a concert on the wrong day or month; be very early for a plane because you thought it left in the morning, not the evening; or miss an appointment because you didn't understand the time.

We depend on the qualifiers a.m. and p.m. to tell us whether the time falls into the first 12 hours of the clock (a.m.) or the second 12 hours (p.m.). To complicate matters, 12:00 is called noon, and 24:00 is called midnight. We also use the colon (:) symbol to separate the hour and minute portions of the time. We do not normally use the period (.) symbol for this. The terms a.m. and p.m. come from Latin: The term a.m. means before (ante) midday, and the term p.m. means after (post) midday. It's just another oddity (idiosyncrasy) to get used to.

Table 6.8 shows the 24-hour clock times next to the double 12-hour clock times.

If you are supposed to meet someone at the movies at 11:00, you might think it is a late morning show, but it may also be a late evening show.

Table 6.8 24-Hour versus 12-Hour Clocks

24-Hour versus 12-Hour Clock Times		*24-Hour versus 12-Hour Clock Times*	
0100 or 1.00	1:00 a.m.	1300 or 13.00	1:00 p.m.
0200 or 2.00	2:00 a.m.	1400 or 14.00	2:00 p.m.
0300 or 3.00	3:00 a.m.	1500 or 15.00	3:00 p.m.
0400 or 4.00	4:00 a.m.	1600 or 16.00	4:00 p.m.
0500 or 5.00	5:00 a.m.	1700 or 17.00	5:00 p.m.
0600 or 6.00	6:00 a.m.	1800 or 18.00	6:00 p.m.
0700 or 7.00	7:00 a.m.	1900 or 19.00	7:00 p.m.
0800 or 8.00	8:00 a.m.	2000 or 20.00	8:00 p.m.
0900 or 9.00	9:00 a.m.	2100 or 21.00	9:00 p.m.
1000 or 10.00	10:00 a.m.	2200 or 22.00	10:00 p.m.
1100 or 11.00	11:00 a.m.	2300 or 23.00	11:00 p.m.
1200 or 12.00	noon	2400 or 24.00	midnight

The absence of a.m. or p.m. makes it hard to tell, doesn't it? If you are supposed to catch a flight at 7:00, you might think it is an 0700 flight, but it may actually be a 7:00 p.m. flight. If you're wrong, you'll be at the airport a very long time!

Clocks that use Roman numerals still exist, so here is the basic conversion system. Remember that these are also 12-hour clocks. Our counting system is called the Arabic number system (our alphabet is the Roman alphabet). Table 6.9 gives you some of the common Roman numerals and their conversions to Arabic (Western) numbers.

Counting in Roman numerals is logical but awkward. Clocks are fairly easy since you just need the first 12 entries in table 6.9.

Movies are a bit harder. If you see a date MCMXLII for a movie, it means the movie was made in (M = 1,000) + (CM = 900) + (XL = 40) + (II = 2), or 1942.

6.9.2 Practice Exercises

Convert the international times to ASM times. Don't forget the a.m. or p.m.

a. 01.15 ________________

b. 1200 ________________

c. 1739 ________________

d. 20.35 ________________

Table 6.9 Roman Numeral to Arabic Number Conversions

1 = I	20 = XX
2 = II	30 = XXX
3 = III	40 = XL (10 less than L)
4 = IV (one less than V)	50 = L
5 = V	60 = LX (10 more than L)
6 = VI (one more than V)	90 = XC (10 less than C)
7 = VII (two more than V)	100 = C
8 = VIII (three more than V)	400 = CD (100 less than D)
9 = IX (one less than X)	500 = D
10 = X	900 = CM (100 less than M)
11 = XI (one more than X)	1,000 = M
12 = XII (two more than X)	
13 = XIII (three more than X)	
14 = XIV (10 plus one less than V)	
15 = XV	

Convert the ASM times to international times. Pay attention to the a.m. and p.m.

e. 4:14 p.m. ______________
f. Midnight ______________
g. 12:20 a.m. ______________
h. 8:28 p.m. ______________

Answers:

a. 1:15 a.m.
b. noon
c. 5:39 p.m.
d. 8:35 p.m.
e. 16.14
f. 24.00
g. 00.20
h. 20.28

6.9.3 The Dates

If the a.m. and p.m. conventions don't cause you problems, the way we write dates almost surely will.

The day comes first. The month comes second. The year is third. The only exceptions you will usually see are customs and immigration forms and legal documents. Customs and immigration forms are normally dated DD/MM/YYYY, but they may be YYYY/MM/DD. Legal documents are usually written as "this 21st day of March, 2005." Sometimes airline documents are written DD/MM/YYYY.

In general, you need to watch the order of your days and months. If you write 03/03/2005, it is the same in either system. If you write 04/03/2005, it is not the next day, it is one full month after the first date!

Another complicating factor is that we normally separate the month, day, and year with "slashes" (/). You probably use periods (.)

Here's why you need to be so careful. If you misunderstand the time (see section 6.9.1), you will probably get somewhere 12 hours too early. If you misunderstand the date, you could miss a lot of very important events (such as meetings and flights).

If you are flying to Europe or Asia and your ticket shows a departure date of 4/3/06, that is probably not 4 March 2006. Instead, it is more likely to be April 3, 2006. In this case, the misunderstanding would get you to the airport a month too soon. If the date were 5/6/08, that is not 5 June 2008. It is May 6, 2008. You would miss your plane by almost a month!

6.9.4 Practice Exercises

These are ASM dates, so the month is first. Write out the following date in words, in ASM style, then in international (DD/MM/YYYY) style.

a. 09/11/07 ____
When will you think your plane leaves if you write this in numbers and don't use the ASM style (day, month, and time)?
b. Your plane leaves at 11 a.m. on Monday, the 6th of July, 2006. _____
Change the following dates to ASM style numbers (MM/DD/YY or MM/DD/YYYY).
c. March 7th, 2006 ____________________________
d. Friday, the 21st of May, 2008 ____________________________

Answers:

a. September 11, 2007; 11.09.07
b. 11:00 a.m, 7/6/06. Not 06/07/06! That's June 6 in ASM.

c. 3/7/06
d. 5/21/08

6.9.5 The Addresses

Addresses involve other unusual things to have to know. First, we don't write our community or subdivision name on our address. If you live in the community called "The Knolls" in the city of Memphis, you leave "The Knolls" off your address.

Next, we put the house, apartment block, or building number first, except in the case of a post office box. Then we put the street name. So, if you live in house number 14 on Mallory Street in The Knolls, Memphis, New Jersey and your zip code is 07001, your address is written:

Alexei and Valentina Gusarov
14 Mallory Street
Memphis, NJ 07001

It is not written:
Gusarov, Alexei and Valentina
The Knolls
Mallory Street 14
07001 Memphis NJ

6.9.6 Practice Exercise

Write your address in your home country in "American style."

6.10 GAMES OF CHANCE

Do you ever plan to go to a casino or just play cards, board games, or dice games with some friends? Then the basic information in chapter 5 will be very useful to you. In this section, we'll look at some real-world situations you might encounter (come across) to help you make more informed choices (decisions). We'll look at odds, probabilities, and similar considerations for these games of chance:

- Slot machines
- Blackjack, or 21
- Dice games (craps, Monopoly, Yahtzee)
- Poker

Each of these games, with the exception of slot machines, has two elements (components): an element of chance and an element of skill. Slots are based (operate, function) on pure chance, using statistically determined (random) numbers programmed into a computer.

Let's start with the game of chance you have least control over—slot machines—then look at the other games you have a bit more (some, limited) control over. (Note: The information in this section is only approximate. If you gamble, always be careful and know your limits!)

6.10.1 Slot Machines

You have no control over the outcome with slot machines. The results are based on random number generation and statistics. Slot machines are "preprogrammed," so the desired (expected) results will occur. These are not the results *you* desire; they are the results the *casinos* desire. There are laws that require slot machines to pay a certain percentage of the money they take in to the people who play them. That is the reason slots pay any money at all.

If you are playing a slot machine and the casino signs claim "93% payouts," that does not mean you will get 93% of your money back or win 93% of the time. Slot machine payouts are much like weather forecasts. If the machine pays out 93%, that means that over some period of time, all the machines of the same type will pay 93% of the money they take in. This money may be paid by one machine (a big payout!), several machines, many machines, or all the machines (in small amounts). You may get several big payouts in a row (in sequence) from one machine. You may put hundreds of dollars in one or more (several) machines and get little of your money back.

The bottom line is that if 10,000 people each put $100 into 10,000 slot machines, and the group of slot machines pays out 93%, here's what happens: The machines will pay 93% of $1,000,000 (10,000 people · $100 · 93%) or $930,000. The machines will pay this money in a combination of ways. Many people will put in \$100 and win nothing. Some people will put in \$100 and win a bit more than \$100. A few people will put in \$100 and win thousands. A very few people (one or two) will put in \$100 and win tens or even hundreds of thousands.

With slot machines, the result is completely predetermined. All you can decide is which machine to use (play) and how many coins to put in each time. Shaking (or banging, tilting, or tipping) the machine will not change the results. Changing machines will not really matter, either.

6.10.2 Practice Exercise

a. You are at a major casino. You have \$50 you are planning to use at (in) the slot machines. The machines promise 89% payouts. How much money should you expect to win or lose?

Answer:

a. Since you have no control over the performance of the slot machine, you should plan to lose all \$50. The only way you might reduce your losses is to keep all payouts (even the very small ones) and don't put them back into the slot machine hoping for "the big one" (that is, a big payout). Using this approach, you will leave with at least some of your original \$50, and may even win a bit (a few dollars). It is always possible you could win a lot of money, but it is very unlikely.

6.10.3 Blackjack or 21

This is one of the games that you have the most control over. If you apply the basics of probability, you have a very good chance of winning more money than you lose. If you gamble recklessly by taking illogical chances, you will probably lose your money.

Go back and look at the charts in chapter 5 ("Probability and Statistics"). As you can see, there is an equal chance of drawing any single card in a deck with 52 cards. However, once you have drawn a card, there is a 0 percent chance of drawing that card. The odds of drawing any of the remaining cards is now 1 in 51 rather than 1 in 52. These decreasing odds are the basis for single-deck (one-deck) blackjack. If you are playing with multiple decks, the basic considerations are still the same, though.

The most important thing to know is when the dealer must take another card and when the dealer must "stand" or not take another card. Casinos use one of two approaches: "Stand" (stay) on 16, and stand on 17. You only get to see one of the two cards the dealer has—but the dealer gets to see both of your cards. You need (have) to make your decisions based on the one card you can see (observe) in the dealer's hand.

So, what can you do? Let's assume you are playing at a casino where the dealer must stand on 17. That means if the cards he or she has total 16 or less, the dealer *must* take another card, unless you take another card (or several cards) and your cards total more than 21. If that's the case, you lose.

If you can see that the dealer has one card that is less than 7, you know the dealer must take another card. There is no other card (the card you can't see) that could make the total more than 16. What does that mean? Let's look at the possibilities (probabilities) in table 6.10. If the dealer already has the first card and draws the second card, an "X" indicates the dealer will stay at or under 21. A "0" indicates the dealer will go over 21. The suit (diamond, spade, club, or heart) does not matter.

The dealer has more chances to win (or not go over 21) than to lose (go over 21). In fact, 115 of the possible 169 card combinations are in the dealer's favor. Of course, this is not completely precise since you and any

Table 6.10 Card Probabilities: Blackjack, Dealer Odds

	Ace	*2*	*3*	*4*	*5*	*6*	*7*	*8*	*9*	*10*	*Jack*	*Queen*	*King*
Ace	X	X	X	X	X	X	X	X	X	X	X	X	X
2	X	X	X	X	X	X	X	X	X	X	X	X	X
3	X	X	X	X	X	X	X	X	X	X	X	X	X
4	X	X	X	X	X	X	X	X	X	X	X	X	X
5	X	X	X	X	X	X	X	X	X	X	X	X	X
6	X	X	X	X	X	X	X	X	X	0	0	0	0
7	X	X	X	X	X	X	X	X	0	0	0	0	0
8	X	X	X	X	X	X	X	0	0	0	0	0	0
9	X	X	X	X	X	X	0	0	0	0	0	0	0
10	X	X	X	X	X	0	0	0	0	0	0	0	0
Jack	X	X	X	X	X	0	0	0	0	0	0	0	0
Queen	X	X	X	X	X	0	0	0	0	0	0	0	0
King	X	X	X	X	X	0	0	0	0	0	0	0	0

other players have some of these cards. However, it is good enough that you should be able to decide whether to take another card.

If you have 16 or less for your two cards, you can use table 6.10 to decide if you should take another card. You need to adjust it for each situation. Those adjustments are shown in tables 6.11 through 6.16.

If *you* have 17 or higher, it is almost always better to stand rather than take another card. It doesn't matter what the dealer has. The likelihood of drawing a four or lower (the only cards that won't cause you to exceed 21) is low. Only 16 of 52 cards are 4 or lower. That means that you have a 69% chance of losing because 16 cards are okay, but 36 are not: 36 ÷ 52 = 0.69, or 69%.

In table 6.11, the "X" indicates (shows) cards that will not put your total over 21. The "0" shows cards that will put you over 21. Only 12 of 52 cards will cause you to lose (go over 21), so 77% of the cards will give you a total of 21 or less. You should probably take another card.

In table 6.12, the "X" indicates (shows) cards that will not put your total over 21. The "0" shows cards that will put you over 21. Only 16 of 52 cards will cause you to lose (go over 21), so 69% of the cards will give you a total of 21 or less. You should probably take another card.

In table 6.13, the "X" indicates (shows) cards that will not put your total over 21. The "0" shows cards that will put you over 21. Only 24 of

Table 6.11 Odds of Losing When Your 2 Cards Total 12 and You Draw Another Card

	Ace	*2*	*3*	*4*	*5*	*6*	*7*	*8*	*9*	*10*	*Jack*	*Queen*	*King*
Spade	X	X	X	X	X	X	X	X	X	0	0	0	0
Club	X	X	X	X	X	X	X	X	X	0	0	0	0
Diamond	X	X	X	X	X	X	X	X	X	0	0	0	0
Heart	X	X	X	X	X	X	X	X	X	0	0	0	0

Table 6.12 Odds of Losing When Your 2 Cards Total 13 and You Draw Another Card

	Ace	*2*	*3*	*4*	*5*	*6*	*7*	*8*	*9*	*10*	*Jack*	*Queen*	*King*
Spade	X	X	X	X	X	X	X	X	0	0	0	0	0
Club	X	X	X	X	X	X	X	X	0	0	0	0	0
Diamond	X	X	X	X	X	X	X	X	0	0	0	0	0
Heart	X	X	X	X	X	X	X	X	0	0	0	0	0

Table 6.13 Odds of Losing When Your 2 Cards Total 14 and You Draw Another Card

	Ace	*2*	*3*	*4*	*5*	*6*	*7*	*8*	*9*	*10*	*Jack*	*Queen*	*King*
Spade	X	X	X	X	X	X	X	0	0	0	0	0	0
Club	X	X	X	X	X	X	X	0	0	0	0	0	0
Diamond	X	X	X	X	X	X	X	0	0	0	0	0	0
Heart	X	X	X	X	X	X	X	0	0	0	0	0	0

52 cards will cause you to lose (go over 21), so 54% of the cards will give you a total of 21 or less. You may or may not want to take another card.

In table 6.14, the "X" indicates (shows) cards that will not put your total over 21. The "0" shows cards that will put you over 21. Since 28 of 52 cards will cause you to lose (go over 21), only 46% of the cards will give you a total of 21 or less. You should probably not take another card.

In table 6.15, the "X" indicates (shows) cards that will not put your total over 21. The "0" shows cards that will put you over 21. Since 32 of 52 cards will cause you to lose (go over 21), only 62% of the cards will give you a total of 21 or less. You should probably not take another card.

In table 6.16, the "X" indicates (shows) cards that will not put your total over 21. The "0" shows cards that will put you over 21. Since 36 of 52 cards will cause you to lose (go over 21), only 31% of the cards will give you a total of 21 or less. You should not take another card.

Table 6.14 Odds of Losing When Your 2 Cards Total 15 and You Draw Another Card

	Ace	*2*	*3*	*4*	*5*	*6*	*7*	*8*	*9*	*10*	*Jack*	*Queen*	*King*
Spade	X	X	X	X	X	X	0	0	0	0	0	0	0
Club	X	X	X	X	X	X	0	0	0	0	0	0	0
Diamond	X	X	X	X	X	X	0	0	0	0	0	0	0
Heart	X	X	X	X	X	X	0	0	0	0	0	0	0

Table 6.15 Odds of Losing When Your 2 Cards Total 16 and You Draw Another Card

	Ace	*2*	*3*	*4*	*5*	*6*	*7*	*8*	*9*	*10*	*Jack*	*Queen*	*King*
Spade	X	X	X	X	X	0	0	0	0	0	0	0	0
Club	X	X	X	X	X	0	0	0	0	0	0	0	0
Diamond	X	X	X	X	X	0	0	0	0	0	0	0	0
Heart	X	X	X	X	X	0	0	0	0	0	0	0	0

Table 6.16 Odds of Losing When Your 2 Cards Total 17 and You Draw Another Card

	Ace	*2*	*3*	*4*	*5*	*6*	*7*	*8*	*9*	*10*	*Jack*	*Queen*	*King*
Spade	X	X	X	X	0	0	0	0	0	0	0	0	0
Club	X	X	X	X	0	0	0	0	0	0	0	0	0
Diamond	X	X	X	X	0	0	0	0	0	0	0	0	0
Heart	X	X	X	X	0	0	0	0	0	0	0	0	0

When you have 18 or higher showing, you should almost never take another card. The odds (chances, probability, likelihood) of losing are very high.

6.10.4 Practice Exercises

a. If you have a total of 14 for your first 2 cards in blackjack, should you take another card? Explain why or why not.
b. If the dealer has a jack showing, how likely do you think it is that the card you can't see is a 7 or higher? Do you think the dealer will have to draw another card? Why or why not?

The answers are subjective.

a. You probably should draw another card since 28 of the cards are in your favor. However, if the dealer has a 10 or higher showing, you may not want to take another card. You may want to gamble that the dealer has to take another card and will lose; this is not a good choice, though.
b. Since there are 28 cards that would be a 7 or higher, there is a good chance that the dealer will not have to take another card.

6.10.5 Dice Games

With games involving dice, the odds of something happening (occurring) or not happening are the same each time you roll (throw) the dice. One roll of the dice has no bearing (relationship) to previous (past) or future (upcoming) rolls.

When you are using one die ("dice" is plural, and "die" is singular), the odds (chances) of getting a 1, 2, 3, 4, 5, or 6 are equal. You have a 1 in 6 chance to roll any of these. If you roll a 3 and then roll again, you might get any of the 6 possibilities.

Table 5.4 in chapter 5 showed you the likelihood (odds) of getting each combination of 2 dice. You need to keep in mind that it is far less likely (probable) that you will roll a 2 (1 on each die) or a 12 (6 on each die) than it is that you will roll a 7 (since there are several ways to get a 7). If a game requires you to roll once to get a total, then keep rolling until you get a 7, then keep rolling until you get the total from your first roll without getting another total (such as 11), you need to know the odds.

The game we just described is a version of craps—a very popular casino game. It is also the game a skilled (experienced, thoughtful) player has the best chance of winning. If your first roll gives you a combination that is less common (2, 3, or 12), you have a lower chance to roll that combination before you roll an 11. If your first roll gives you a more frequent combination such as 5, 6, 7, or 8, you are more likely to roll that combination before you roll an 11.

In the game Yahtzee, you use 5 dice and try to roll certain combinations. If you need to roll three of the same number, you have five dice to do so. If you get two of the number you need, you can pick up the three incorrect dice and roll them again. If you still don't have three of the same number, you can pick up as many of the dice as you wish and roll one more time. The more specific the combination you must roll, the harder it is. If you need to roll three of something and get three tries, your chances are pretty good (high). If you need to roll five of the same number, your chances are not very high. A strategy (skill) in this game is to try to get the harder (less likely) combinations first.

Monopoly is another game that relies on both skill and rolling dice. In this game, you only use two dice. There are certain blocks you want to land on, and some you want to avoid. There is not much you can do except hope for good (favorable) rolls of the dice and build lots of hotels so you can bankrupt your fellow players!

6.10.6 Poker

Poker is a game of skill and chance. You can only win consistently (regularly) if you understand the odds of getting certain combinations. Let's assume that you are playing "draw" poker with five cards. You are allowed to replace from one to all five cards and get new ones. Let's also assume that there is only a single deck of cards being used. You do not know what cards the other players have drawn at first or replaced. We are not using "wild" cards.

Table 6.17 shows the possible cards in a deck.

If you have drawn the poker hand shown in figure 6.18, you have several choices.

You have two jacks (a pair) and two aces (another pair). Two pairs is a decent hand. You could replace the 10 of clubs to see if you can get another jack or another ace. Since there are 4 aces and 4 jacks in a single deck of cards, and you have 2 of each, there are at most 2 of each left. You do not know if someone else has these cards. Still, you will not lose anything by trying to get one of these 4 possible cards. You might end up with 3 of a kind, and that is more valuable than 2 pairs.

You might also try for a straight, which is 5 cards in sequence. You could try to get 5 in the same suit (all clubs, for example). You could even try for a royal flush (the 10, jack, queen, king, and ace in the same suit). The royal flush is very rare.

If you decide to try for the straight, you might as well try for the royal flush. You would keep the 10 and jack of clubs since they are the only two cards in the same suit. You would need the queen, king, and ace of clubs

Table 6.17 Possible Cards in a Deck

	Ace	*2*	*3*	*4*	*5*	*6*	*7*	*8*	*9*	*10*	*Jack*	*Queen*	*King*
Spade	X	X	X	X	X	X	X	X	X	X	X	X	X
Club	X	X	X	X	X	X	X	X	X	X	X	X	X
Diamond	X	X	X	X	X	X	X	X	X	X	X	X	X
Heart	X	X	X	X	X	X	X	X	X	X	X	X	X

- Ace of spades
- Jack of clubs
- Jack of diamonds
- Ace of hearts
- 10 of clubs

Figure 6.18 Sample Poker Hand

to have a royal flush. There are only three cards that will work, and you don't know what cards the other players have. The chances (odds) of getting these three cards are not good at all.

You could also keep the 10 and jack of clubs and try for a straight all in clubs or in any mix of suits. A straight with all clubs would need to be 7 8 9 10 J, 8 9 10 J Q, 9 10 J Q K, or 10 J Q K A (the royal flush). There are 6 cards that might work, but not in every combination. Your odds of getting the cards you need are 6 out of the number of cards left, and others may have the cards you need. And not all of the cards will work. If you get the 8, J, Q, and K of clubs you still win something, but less than if the cards were in sequence.

You could also try for any straight—the cards must be in order, but the suits do not have to be the same. In that case, there are six cards in each suit (8, 9, J, Q, K, A) that could work, but not in every combination. If you drew a 9 of clubs, jack of hearts, and queen of diamonds, you would only have one pair (the jack of clubs you kept and the jack of hearts you drew). If you drew the 9 of clubs, queen of diamonds, king of hearts, and ace of spades, you would have a straight and would win something. Of course, other players may also draw the cards you need.

You would probably be best off keeping the 2 pairs and trying to draw a third ace or jack.

6.10.7 Practice Exercise

a. You have the following cards: 7 of diamonds, 7 of spades, 3 of diamonds, 5 of diamonds, and ace of clubs. What are your choices? What choice makes the most sense to you? Sit down with someone who knows the rules and strategies of poker and talk about this exercise.

There are many possible answers. You would probably keep the two sevens and swap out the other three cards in hopes of getting another seven. You might also keep the three diamonds and trade the other two cards in hopes of getting two more diamonds.

Answers to End-of-Chapter Homework Problems

CHAPTER 1

Fill in the blank with a correct (appropriate) word or phrase:

1 .5 yards is a bit less than, about the same as 5 meters.
2. 28 grams is about the same as, a bit less than, close to 1 ounce.
3. 1 mile is more than 1 kilometer.
4. 5 liters is more than 1 gallon.
5. 500 ml is about, close to, a bit more than 1 pint.
6. One c. is about the same as, close to, a bit less than 250 ml.
7. 5,000 ft is more than 1,000 meters.
8. 25°C is the same as 75°F.
9. 2 kg is about the same as, nearly the same as, close to the same as 4.5 lbs.
10. 10 square meters is about the same as, nearly the same as 100 square ft.
11. 1 square yard is a bit less than, close to 1 square meter.
12. 100 kg is a bit more than, more than 200 lbs.
13. 24 oz. is the same as 3 c.
14. 2 quarts is a bit less than 2 l.
15. 2 gallons is the same as 8 qts.
16. 4 pints is the same as 1/2 of 1 gal.
17. 1 liter is a bit more than 4 c.
18. 167 cm is about the same as, nearly the same as 66 in.
19. 6′7″ is about, close to, a bit more than 2 m.
20. 30 cm is about the same as, close to 1 foot.

Convert from metric to ASM. Use the appropriate qualifier (about, more than, less than, close to, the same as).

21. 4 liters is about 1 gal., about 4 qts., about 8 pints, about 16 cups (or you can say a bit more than 1 gal., 4 qts., 8 pts., or 16 c.).
22. 5 cm is about 2″, about 2 inches.
23. 250 ml is a bit more than 1 c, about 1 cup.
24. 3 km is a bit less than 2 miles, about 2 mi.
25. 5,000 m is about three miles, a bit more than 5,000 yds., a bit more than 3 mi.
26. 500 g is about 1 lb., a bit more than 1 pound.
27. 4 kg is about 9 lbs., less than 10 pounds.
28. 28°C is the same as 82°F.
29. 0°C is the same as 32°F, the same as freezing.
30. 1,600 m is about 1 mile, about 1,750 yds.
31. 400 m is a bit more than 400 yds., about 1/4 mi.
32. 5 ml is about 1 tsp.
33. 15 ml is about 1 tbs.
34. 1,000 ml is about one qt., a bit more than 1 quart, about 2 pts., a bit more than 2 pints, about 4 c., a bit more than 4 cups.
35. 1/2 liter is about 2 cups, a bit more than 2 c., about 1 pt., a bit more than 1 pint.
36. 500 km is about 300 miles, a bit more than 300 miles.
37. 2,500 m is about 8,250′, a bit more than 2,500 yds.
38. 450 dl is more than 1 gal., about 5 qts.
39. 50 ml is a bit less than 2 ounces.
40. 1.6 km is about 1 mile.

Convert from ASM to metric:

41. 1 mi. is about 1.6 km.
42. 212°F is the same as, exactly 100°C.
43. 350°F is about 177°C.
44. 1 qt. is a bit less than 1 l, about 1 liter.
45. 1 c. is a bit less than 250 ml, about 250 milliliters.
46. 1 pint is about 1/2 liter, a bit less than 500 ml, about 500 ml, a bit less than 1/2 l.
47. 1 lb. is 454 grams, about 500 g, a bit less than 500 grams.

48. 5′11″ is about 180 cm, a bit more than 177 cm.
49. 1/2 c. is about 250 ml, a bit less than 250 ml, 1/4 l, a bit less than 1/4 l.
50. 1 gal. is about 4 liters, a bit less than 4 liters.
51. 4 oz. is about 125 ml, a bit less than 125 ml, a bit less than 1/8 liter.
52. 800 sf is about 80 square meters.
53. 5 acres is about 2 hectares.
54. 30 mph is about 50 kph, a bit less than 50 kph.
55. 1,000 mi. is about 1,600 km.
56. 2,000′ is about 600 m.
57. 2,000 yds. is about 1800 m, less than 2,000 m.
58. 150 lbs. is about 68 kg, a bit less than 70 kg.
59. 1/2 mi. is a bit less than 1 km, a bit less than 1,000 m.
60. 5 lbs. is more than 2 kg, about 2.25 kg.
61. 2 tsp is about 10 ml.
62. 4 tbs is about 60 ml.
63. 11

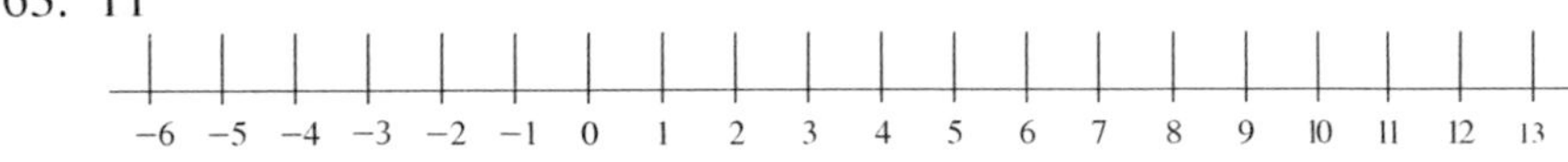

64. −3

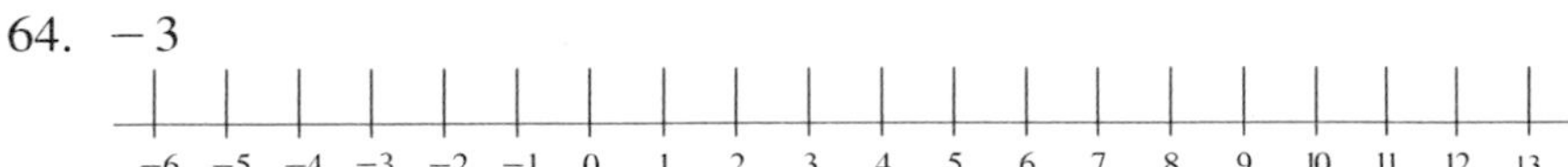

65. 3

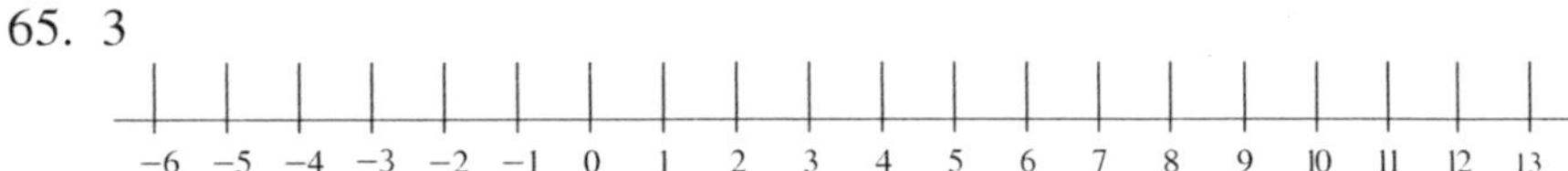

66. 11

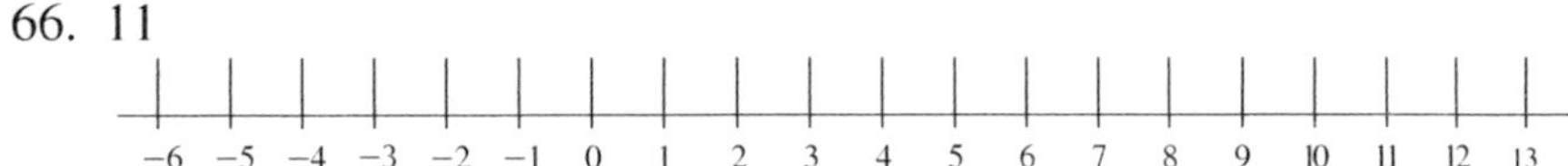

67. 7

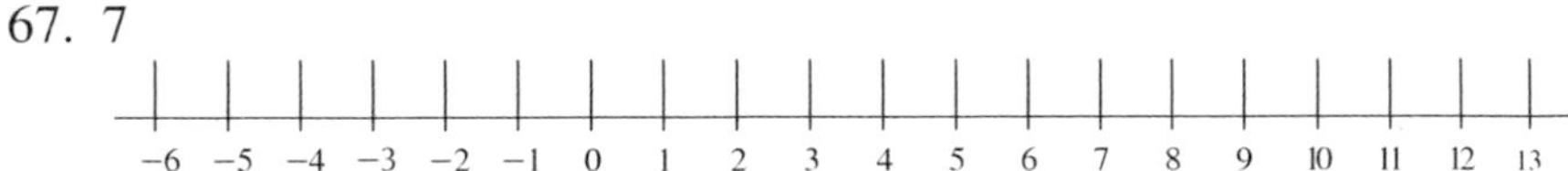

68. −6

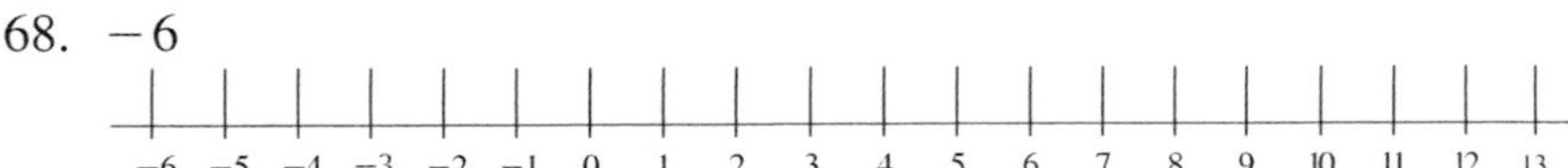

69. 1

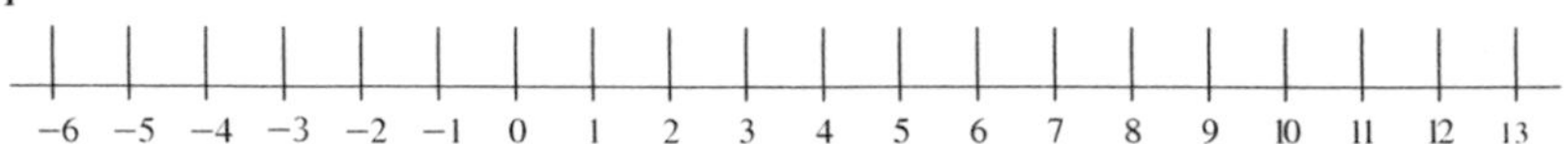

70. −6

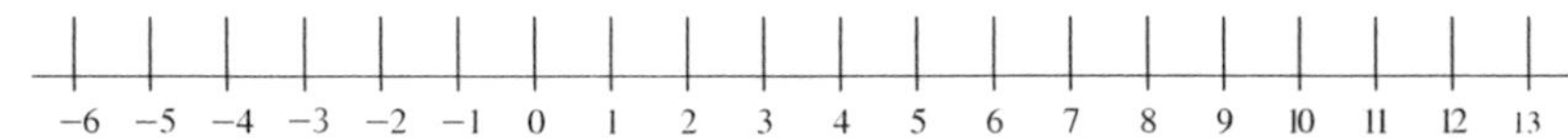

71. $5 + (7-3)(5-6) =$

   a. Perform the operations inside the parentheses (subtraction in both cases): $5 + (4)(-1)$
   b. Clear the parentheses by performing the operations indicated (multiplication): $5 + (-4)$
   c. Solve the problem: $5 + (-4)$ is the same as $5 - 4 = 1$

72. $b(c + a) + bc + ba =$

   a. You can't do anything about adding c + a since you don't know what either one represents.
   b. Apply b to each variable in the parentheses to clear the parentheses: $(b \cdot c) + (b \cdot a) + bc + ba$
   c. Perform the multiplication and remove the parentheses: $bc + ba + bc + ba$
   d. Collect the like (similar) terms and add them (Commutative Property of Addition): $bc + bc + ba + ba = 2bc + 2ba$

73. $(14)(6 \div 2) + 4 - (-9) =$

   a. Perform the operation inside the parentheses: $(6 \div 2) = 3$, so the equation becomes: $(14)(3) + 4 - (-9)$
   b. Perform the multiplication: $14 \cdot 3 = 42$, so the equation becomes: $42 + 4 - (-9)$
   c. A negative number subtracted from a positive number is a larger positive number. You can change the minus and negative signs to plus (+) signs, and the equation becomes: $42 + 4 + 9 = 55$

74. $(15 \cdot 4)(4 \div 2) - 7 + (-9) - 18 =$

a. Perform the multiplication and division operations inside each set of parentheses: $15 \cdot 4 = 60$, and $4 \div 2 = 2$, so the equation becomes $(60 \cdot 2) - 7 + (-9) - 18$
b. Perform the remaining multiplication operation: $60 \cdot 2 = 120$, so the equation becomes $120 - 7 + (-9) - 18$
c. Remember that a negative number added to a positive number is the same as subtracting the negative number from the positive number, so the equation becomes $120 - 7 - 9 - 18$
d. Now you can solve the equation, being careful of the negative signs: $120 - 7 - 9 - 18 = 86$ (Note that $-7 - 9 - 18 = -34$, so $120 - 34 = 86$.)

75.

a. About 800 miles (70 is OK)
b. About 62 mph on average
c. About 13.5 gallons
d. About 28 miles per gallon
e. Yes
f. Twice
g. About 29
h. About 9 oz.; just over 1/2 lb.
i. About 3.5 oz.
j. About 11 oz. or 2/3 lb.

CHAPTER 2

2.4.1 Rounding Whole Numbers

1. 50
2. 5,700
3. 0
4. 100
5. 880

6. 15,000
7. 345,200
8. 345,000
9. 350,000
10. 300,000
11. 10
12. 1,090
13. 1,100
14. 960
15. 1,000
16. 4,550
17. 4,500
18. 5,000
19. 3,400,000
20. 3,432,500

2.4.2 Rounding Numbers with a Decimal Component

21. 0.03
22. 3.5
23. 0.71
24. 46.0
25. 100.99
26. 101
27. 0.745
28. 0.74
29. 510
30. 509.67
31. 0.0002
32. 0
33. 0.5
34. 4
35. 4.1
36. 4.098
37. 4.0987
38. 0.61

39. 0.606
40. 0.6

2.4.3 Estimating and Approximating

41. 450 square feet
42. 50 square yards, 45 square meters, yes
43. 7 or 8 yards
44. 8 or 9 hours, but you only have 7 hours until the concert starts
45. About 550 (544) square feet of wall space
46. 2 gallons of paint
47. Maybe there is enough. Since both wall dimensions were rounded up, you probably have enough paint.
48.

    a. Used about 3 gallons so far
    b. About 12 gallons left
    c. 396 miles if all goes well
    d. Filling up would be a good idea!

49. If you have estimated incorrectly or your car uses more fuel than you think, you will run out of gas in a very unpleasant place.
50. About 50°C

2.4.4 Breaking the Rounding, Estimating, and Approximating Rules

51. It is better to get the price for 55 square yards. Then the estimate you get will be higher rather than lower than the actual price.
52. If you round to the nearest hundred, you will think you ate 400 calories, so in theory you will eat less food and lose weight faster.
53.

    a. 350
    b. 300
    c. 400

2.4.5 Real-World Word Problems

54.

a. Table: 60 inches; bed: 80 inches; sofa: 90 inches
b. Table window space: 60 to 64 inches
   Bedroom window space: 70 to 74 inches
   Living room window space: 80 to 84 inches
c. Your sofa may not fit. The range of possible exact measurements (before rounding) is 90 to 94 inches. Your sofa is 93 inches. If the exact measurement is 90 inches, 91 inches, or 92 inches, your sofa will block the window. The other measurements are fine.
d. You will need to ask for the exact measurement of the space between the living room windows.

55.

a. Neck: 17 inches
   Chest: 40 inches
   Waist: 40 inches
   Arm length: 33 inches
   Leg length: 30 inches
b. Neck: 16.5 inches
   Chest: 43 inches
   Waist: 35 inches
   Arm length: 33 inches
   Leg length: 34 inches
c. If Matthew rounds to the nearest ten, none of the clothing measurements will be of any use.

CHAPTER 3

1. Seventeen
2. Thirty-seven
3. Eighty-two

4. Ninety
5. One hundred one
6. One hundred seventy
7. One hundred twenty-four
8. Two hundred ninety-seven
9. Three thousand four
10. Four thousand ninety-six
11. Six thousand three hundred thirty-three
12. Eleven thousand two hundred one
13. Fifteen thousand six hundred seventy-four
14. Nineteen thousand five
15. Seventy-six thousand three hundred eighty
16. One hundred one thousand four hundred fifty-six
17. Three hundred fifty-six thousand eight hundred ninety-six
18. Four hundred seven thousand seven hundred
19. Five hundred sixty-one thousand eight hundred two
20. Three million four hundred fifty-six thousand nine hundred ninety-nine
21. Eight million four hundred one
22. Seven million four hundred thousand three hundred ninety-six
23. Fourteen million nine hundred seventy-six thousand three hundred thirty-four
24. Thirty-four million five hundred sixty-seven thousand nine hundred
25. Sixty-four million four hundred thousand four hundred fifty-four
26. One hundred twenty-four million three hundred thirty-three thousand eight hundred ninety-eight
27. 13
28. 27
29. 90
30. 143
31. 517
32. 704
33. 5,067
34. 3,697
35. 12,555
36. 13,406
37. 81,312

38. 63,001
39. 421,631
40. 100,091
41. 210,400
42. 5,002,017
43. 7,333,400
44. 8,507,063
45. 44,762,527
46. Four fifths
47. Three hundred fifty-six and three fourth or three hundred fifty-six and three quarters
48. Five and three hundred fifty-four one thousandths
49. Eight and one eighth
50. Three hundred fifty-six and three sixteenths
51. Five and nine hundred two one thousandths
52. Seventy-eight thousand six hundred fifty-four one hundred thousandths
53. Ninety-eight and nine thousand eight hundred ninety-eight ten thousandths
54. Ninety-eight one millionths
55. Thirty-four and ten thousand eighty-eight one millionths
56. Seventy-seven percent
57. One hundred forty-three percent
58. Seventeen percent
59. Three thousand four hundred sixty-one percent
60. Five point two percent
61. 0.77
62. 1.43
63. 0.17
64. 34.61
65. 0.052
66. 80%
67. 167%
68. 50%
69. 225%
70. About 43%
71. Sixty-five degrees Fahrenheit

72. Twenty-two degrees Celsius
73. 0.002
74. 5.0017
75. 4 3/4
76. 2,076.03487
77. 98 5/16
78. 2,107,621.33
79. 1/2
80. 71 33/100
81. 5/64 (this one is a bit tricky)
82. 99/1,000
83. 463%
84. 1,000%
85. 62.5%
86. 18%
87. 94%
88. 25°C
89. 75°C
90.

Michaela Smets
134 Main Street
Devonville, MA 99999

Date: March 22, 2006[4]

[5] Pay to the order of Public Service of the East Amount 123.47[6]

Amount in words: One hundred twenty-three and 47/100 dollars [7]

[8] Memo Account 305–999–001 Signed *Michaela Smets* [9]

91.

a. $4,000
b. $1,226
c. 30.65%
d. $2,774

CHAPTER 4

Section 4.1 Fractions

1. 5/4 · 5/4 = 25/16 = 1 9/16
2. 4/5 · 5/4 = 20/20 = 1
3. 1 5/9 · 6/7 = 14/9 · 6/7 = 84/63 = 1 21/63 = 1 1/3
4. 2/9 · 99 1/2 = 2/9 ·198/2 = 396/18 = 22
5. 3 3/5 · 4 4/7 = 18/5 · 32/7 = 576/35 = 16 16/35
6. 1/2 · 3/4 = 3/8
7. 36 1/3 · 1/3 = 108/3 · 1/3 = 108/9 = 12
8. 6/7 · 9/3 = 63/21 = 3
9. 5 · 1/8 = 5/1 · 1/8 = 5/8
10. 4 7/8 · 13 = 39/8 · 13/1 = 507/8 = 63 3/8
11. 4/5 ÷ 4/5 = 4/5 · 5/4 = 1
12. 17 ÷ 1/2 = 17/1 · 2/1 = 34/1 = 34
13. 3 1/3 ÷ 6 1/6 = 10/3 · 6/37 = 60/111
14. 3/4 ÷ 7/8 = 3/4 · 8/7 = 24/28 = 6/7
15. 14 1/4 ÷ 7 1/8 = 57/4 · 8/57 = 8/4 = 2
16. 7/8 ÷ 2 = 7/8 · 1/2 = 7/16
17. 8 1/7 ÷ 6 1/9 = 57/7 · 9/55 = 513/385 = 1 128/385
18. 1/4 ÷ 1/2 = 1/4 · 2/1 = 2/4 = 1/2
19. 6 1/5 ÷ 8 = 31/5 · 1/8 = 31/40
20. 1 ÷ 9/10 = 1/1 · 10/9 = 10/9 = 1 1/9
21. 4/9 + 7/8 = 32/72 + 63/72 = 95/72 = 1 23/72
22. 4 3/4 + 4/5 = 95/20 + 16/20 = 111/20 = 5 11/20
23. 5 + 7/8 = 40/8 + 7/8 = 47/8 = 5 7/8
24. 1/2 + 5 3/16 = 16/32 + 166/32 = 182/32 = 5 22/32 = 5 11/16
25. 1 1/2 + 3 1/6 = 18/12 + 39/12 = 57/12 = 4 9/12 = 4 3/4
26. 7 1/2 + 4 1/2 = 15/2 + 9/2 = 24/2 = 12
27. 19 3/4 + 3 4/7 = 553/28 + 100/28 = 653/28 = 23 9/28
28. 6 1/8 + 4 2/3 = 147/24 + 112/24 = 259/24 = 10 19/24
29. 4 1/2 + 3 1/3 + 5 1/2 = 54/12 + 40/12 + 66/12 = 160/12 = 13 4/12 = 13 1/3
30. 6 1/8 + 9 1/3 + 11/2 = 294/48 + 448/48 + 264/48 = 1,006/48 = 20 46/48 = 20 23/24
31. 3/4 − 1/2 = 6/8 − 4/8 = 2/8 = 1/4
32. 4 4/7 − 1 1/2 = 64/14 − 21/14 = 43/14 = 3 1/14

33. 5 − 1 1/2 = 10/2 − 3/2 = 7/2 = 3 1/2
34. 7 1/8 − 8 1/4 = 228/32 − 264/32 = −36/32 = −1 4/32 = −1 1/8
35. 4 4/29 − 3 1/2 = 240/58 − 203/58 = 37/58
36. 3/39 − 1/13 = 39/507 − 39/507 = 0
37. 4 1/8 − 6 3/8 = 33/8 − 51/8 = −18/8 = −2 2/8 = −2 1/4
38. 1 3/4 − 1 1/2 = 14/8 − 12/8 = 2/8 = 1/4
39. 2 1/3 − 1 1/2 − 7/8 = 112/48 − 72/48 − 42/48 = −2/48 = −1/24
40. 8 − 6 1/6 − 1 1/2 = 96/12 − 74/12 − 18/12 = 4/12 = 1/3

Section 4.2 Decimals

41. 10.54
42. 0.542
43. 48.4
44. 2.32
45. 0.25
46. 1.96
47. .667
48. .00003
49. 1,085.99
50. 13.471

Section 4.3 Ratios

51. There are 6 ways to get a 7 [(1, 6), (2, 5), (3, 4), (4, 3), (5, 2), and (6, 1)]. There are 36 possible combinations of two dice. If 6 of those combinations are 7s, then the ratio of 7s to other options is 6:30, which reduces to 1:5.
52. 20 mpg; 1:20
53. 27.5; 1:27.5
54. #52
55. #53
56.

    a. Pay for three shirts, the fourth one is free.

b. 3
c. 1:3
d. 4:3
e. 4:1

Section 4.4 Percents

57. 160%
58. 15% wrong, 85% right
59. 45.67%
60. 30.3%
61. 29%
62. 80%
63. 25%
64. 970%
65.

    a. $336
    b. $10,836
    c. $422.44
    d. $11,269.44

66. 167%, 166.7%, or 166.67%
67. 4.2 is larger
68. They are exactly the same.
69. 65% is a bit smaller
70. 25.2%

CHAPTER 5

Section 5.3.1—Understanding Probability

1. The chances of rain on any particular day are fairly low. On average, it will rain (shower) on one of every five days with this forecast. At the same time, there could be many days when there is no rain, then several days when it rains every day. At the end of the year, it will probably have rained about 20% of the days with this forecast.

2. Since there are 52 cards, you have a 1 in 52 chance of drawing one specific (particular) card the first time. That is a ratio of 1:51 since 51 of the cards would not be the one you want.
3. Since you have drawn 4 cards, there are only 48 cards left (remaining). Your chances of drawing one specific card are 1 in 48. That is a ratio of 1:47 since 47 of the cards are not the one you want.
4. Since there are 52 cards, you have a 1 in 52 chance of drawing one specific (particular) card the first time. That is a ratio of 1:51 since 51 of the cards would not be the one you want.
5. Since you have drawn 6 cards, there are only 46 cards left (remaining). Your chances of drawing one specific card are 1 in 46. That is a ratio of 1:45 since 45 of the cards are not the one you want.

Section 5.3.2—Using Probability

6. 1/6
7. 1/6
8. 5/6
9. 4/6
10. Anything is possible. If you roll one die enough times, eventually you will see a pattern. You will see 1/6 of your rolls resulting in a 1, 1/6 of your rolls resulting in a 2, and so forth. For a very small sample (10 rolls), the results above are both possible and probable.
11. Rolling the same number 10 times in a row is possible, but not probable.
12. Rolling a die one time has no effect on future rolls. Each possible option (1, 2, 3, 4, 5, and 6) is available for each roll. This is different from card games since once a card is dealt (used, played), it is not normally available again.
13.
    a. Yes, the information is very useful. It tells you exactly what you needed to know.
    b. You wanted to travel when the chance of rain was low and the chance of temperatures no higher than 85°F was greatest (most likely).
    c. April and May are fairly dry and relatively cool. September might also work.

Appendix A

Conversion Charts: Basic Conversions

UNITS OF MEASUREMENT

Distance, Height, and Length	**Conversions/Comparisons**
1 inch (in.) is about	2.5 centimeters (cm) (British: centimetres).
1 centimeter (cm) is about	0.4 inches (in.).
1 foot (ft.) is about	30 centimeters (cm).
1 yard (yd.) is a bit smaller than	1 meter (m) (British: metre).
1 meter is a bit bigger than	1 yard (yd.).
1 yard (yd.) is exactly 3 feet (ft.).	
1 meter (m) is a bit more than	3 feet (ft.).
1 hectare is about	2.5 acres (ac.).
1 acre (ac.) is about	0.4 hectares.
1 mile (mi.) is a bit less than	2 kilometers (km) (British: kilometres).
2 kilometers (km) are a bit more than	1 mile (mi.).
1/2 or 0.5 mile (mi.) is a bit less than	1 kilometer (km).
1 mile (mi.) is exactly	5,280 feet (ft.).
1 mile is about	1,600 meters (m).
6 miles (mi.) is about	10 kilometers (km).
10 kilometers (km) is about	6 miles (mi.).

Weight/Dry Measures	**Conversions/Comparisons**
1 ounce (oz.) is about	28 grams (g).
30 grams (g) is a bit more than	1 ounce (oz.).
4 ounces (oz.) is a bit more than	100 grams (g).
4 ounces (oz.) is exactly	1/4 of 1 pound (lb.).
100 grams (g) is a bit less than	4 ounces (oz.) or 1/4 of 1 pound (lb.).

8 ounces (oz.) is a bit less than	250 grams (g).
8 ounces (oz.) is exactly	1/2 of 1 pound (lb.).
250 grams (g) is a bit more than	1/2 of 1 pound (lb.) or 8 ounces (oz.).
16 ounces (oz.) is a bit less than	500 grams (g).
16 ounces (oz.) is exactly	1 pound (lb.).
1 pound (lb.) is a bit less than	1/2 of 1 kilogram (kg) or 500 grams (g).
1 kilogram (kg) is about	2.2 pounds (lbs.).
2 pounds (lbs.) is a bit less than	1 kilogram (kg).
100 pounds (lbs.) is about	45 kilograms (kg).
50 kilograms (kg) is about	110 pounds (lbs.).
220 pounds (lbs.) is about	100 kilograms (kg).
100 kilograms (kg) is about	220 pounds (lbs.).
1 metric ton (t) (also called "tonne") is about	2,200 pounds (lbs.).
1 AMS ton (t) is about	900 kilograms (kg).

Volume/Liquid Measures	**Conversions/Comparisons**
1 ounce (oz.) is about	30 milliliters (ml).
30 milliliters (ml) is about	1 ounce (oz.).
8 ounces (oz.) is a bit less than	250 milliliters (ml).
8 ounces (oz.) is exactly	1 cup (c.).
1 cup (c.) is a bit less than	250 milliliters (ml).
16 ounces (oz.) is a bit less than	500 milliliters (ml) or 1/2 liter (l).
16 ounces (oz.) is exactly	2 cups (c.) or 1 pint (pt.).
2 cups (c.) is exactly	1 pint (pt.).
1 pint (pt.) or 2 cups (c.) is about	500 milliliters (ml) or 1/2 liter (l).
32 ounces (oz.) is a bit less than	1,000 milliliters (ml) or 1 liter (l).
32 ounces (oz.) is exactly	1 quart (qt.) or 2 pints (pts.).
1 quart (qt.) is a bit less than	1 liter (l).
64 ounces (oz.) is a bit less than	2 liters (l).
64 ounces (oz.) is exactly	1/2 gallon (gal.) or 2 quarts (qts.). or 4 pints (pts.) or 8 cups (c.).
1 gallon (gal.) is less than	4 liters (l).
13 gallons (gal.) is about	50 liters (l).
50 liters (l) is about	13 gallons (gal.).

Temperatures	**Conversions/Comparisons**
0 degrees centigrade (also called Celsius) is exactly	32 degrees Fahrenheit.
32 degrees Fahrenheit is exactly	0 degrees centigrade.
10 degrees centigrade is about	50 degrees Fahrenheit.
50 degrees Fahrenheit is about	10 degrees centigrade.
20 degrees centigrade is about	68 degrees Fahrenheit.
68 degrees Fahrenheit is about	20 degrees centigrade.
25 degrees centigrade is about	75 degrees Fahrenheit.
75 degrees Fahrenheit is about	25 degrees centigrade.
28 degrees centigrade is about	82 degrees Fahrenheit.
82 degrees Fahrenheit is about	28 degrees centigrade.
−40 degrees Fahrenheit is exactly	−40 degrees centigrade.

DISTANCES, HEIGHTS, WIDTHS, LENGTHS, AND CIRCUMFERENCES MEASURES

American Standard Measurements	**Metric Measurements**
No true counterpart	*millimeters* (also written as mm)
inches (abbreviated as in. or ″)	*centimeters* (cm is the short form)
foot (singular), *feet* (plural) (both abbreviated as ft.)	No true counterpart
yard (abbreviated as yd.)	*meter* (short form is m)
mile (mi. is the short form)	*kilometer* (abbreviated km)

WEIGHTS OR DRY MEASURES

American Standard Measurements	**Metric Measurements**
ounce (oz.)	*gram* (g)
pound (lb.)	*kilogram* (kg)
ton (t)	*tonne* (t)

VOLUMES OR LIQUID MEASURES

American Standard Measurements	**Metric Measurements**
teaspoon (tsp)	*milliliter* (ml)
tablespoon (tbs or tbsp)	*milliliter* (ml)
ounce (oz.)	No true counterpart
cup (c.)	No true counterpart
pint (pt.)	No true counterpart
quart (qt.)	*liter* (l)
gallon (gal.)	No true counterpart

TEMPERATURES

American Standard Measurements	**Metric Measurements**
Fahrenheit (°F)	centigrade (or Celsius) (°C)

MORE PRECISE CONVERSIONS TO AND FROM ASM/METRIC

1 in. = 2.54 cm	1 cm = 0.4 in.	1 foot = 30 cm	25 cm = 10 in.
100 cm = 1 m	36 in. = 1 yd.	1 yd. = 0.915 m	1 m = 1.1 yd.
1 km = 1,000 m	1 mi. = 5,280 ft.	1 mi. = 1,760 yds.	1 km = 0.62 mi.
1 mi. = 1.6 km	1 mi. = 1,600 m	2 km = 1.24 mi.	1 oz. = 28.3 g
28.3 g = 1 oz.	1 c. = 8 oz.	1 c. = 225 ml	250 ml = 1.125 c.
2 c. = 1 pt.	16 oz. = 1 pt.	1 pt. = 450 ml	500 ml = 17.4 oz.
1 qt. = 32 oz.	1 qt. = 2 pts.	1 qt. = 4 c.	1 qt. = 0.91 l
1 l = 1.1 qt.	1 l = 1,000 ml	1 qt. = 910 ml	1/2 gal. = 64 oz.
1/2 gal. = 2 qts.	1/2 gal. = 4 pts.	1/2 gal. = 8 c.	1/2 gal. = 1.83 l
2 l = 2.2 qts.	1/2 gal. = 1,830 ml	1 gal. = 128 oz.	1 gal. = 2.5 gal.
1 gal. = 4 qts.	1 gal. = 8 pts.	1 gal. = 16 c.	1 gal. = 3.7 l
4 l = 1.1 gal.	1 gal. = 3,760 ml	1 oz. = 28.3 g	4 oz. = 113.2 g
100 g = 3.5 oz.	8 oz. = 226.4 g	250 g = 9 oz.	16 oz. = 1 lb.
16 oz. = 454 g	500 g = 17.5 oz.	1 lb. = 0.454 kg	1 kg = 2.2 lbs.

2 lbs. = 0.9 kg	1 t = 2,000 lbs. (ASM)	1 t = 1,000 kg (metric)	0°C = 32°F (freezing point of water)
−40°C = −40°F	20°C = 68°F	25°C = 75°F	28°C = 82°F
100°C = 212°F (boiling point of water)	350°F = 176°C (common baking temperature)	400°F = 204°C (common baking temperature)	500°F = 260°C (common pizza-baking temperature)

USEFUL CONVERSION FORMULAS

To convert from Fahrenheit to centigrade:

- Subtract 32 from the temperature in °F.
- Divide the result by 9.
- Multiply the result by 5.

Example:
To convert 212°F to °C:

- 212 − 32 = 180
- 180 ÷ 9 = 20
- 20 · 5 = 100°C

To convert from centigrade to Fahrenheit:

- Divide the temperature in °C by 5.
- Multiply the result by 9.
- Add 32 to the result.

Example:
To convert 28°C to °F:

- 28 ÷ 5 = 5.6
- 5.6 · 9 = 50.4
- 50.4 + 32 = 82.4 (Note how close this is to the approximate conversion in table 1.4.)

To convert from miles to kilometers, multiply the number of miles by 1.62.

Example:

200 mi. · 1.62 = 324 km

To convert from kilometers to miles, multiply the number of kilometers by 0.62.

Example:
200 km · 0.62 = 124 mi.

To convert from inches to centimeters, multiply the number in inches by 2.54.
Example:
50 in. · 2.54 = 127 cm

To convert from centimeters to inches, multiply the number in centimeters by 0.394.
Example:
100 cm · 0.394 = 39.4 in.

To convert from quarts to liters, multiply the number in quarts by 0.91.
Example:
4 qts. · 0.91 = 3.64 l

To convert from liters to quarts, multiply the number in liters by 1.1.
Example:
6 l · 1.1 = 6.6 qts.

To convert from liters to gallons, multiply the number in liters by 0.27.
Example:
4 l · 0.27 = 1.1 gal.

To convert from gallons to liters, multiply the number in gallons by 3.64.
Example:
4 gal. · 3.64 = 14.56 l

To convert from kilograms to pounds, multiply the number in kg by 2.2.
Example:
80 kg · 2.2 = 176 lbs.

To convert from pounds to kilograms, multiply the number in lbs. by 0.45.
Example:
150 lbs. · 0.45 = 67.5 kg

To convert from yards to meters, multiply the number in yards by 0.915.
Example:
5 yds. · 0.915 = 4.58 m

To convert from meters to yards, multiply the number in meters by 1.1.
Example:
10 m · 1.1 = 11 yds.

Appendix B

Mathematical Symbols

Mathematical Symbol	Purpose
$+$	addition, increase in value, plus, more, positive (number, temperature)
$-$	subtraction, decrease in value, minus, less, negative (number, temperature)
( ) or $\times$ or * or $\cdot$	multiplication, times, multiply
$\div$ or / or $\sqrt{}$	division, divided by, divide
$=$	equal to, the same as, equivalent
$\neq$	not equal to, not the same as, different than
$<$	less than, smaller than
$\leqslant$	equal to or less than, the same or smaller
$>$	more than, larger than
$\geqslant$	equal to or greater than, the same or bigger
$\pm$	plus or minus, give or take, either way
$\sim$	approximately
.	decimal point
,	separator for hundreds/thousands, hundred thousands/millions, and so forth
$	dollar sign (U.S. dollar, USD)
¢	cent sign
%	percent
′	foot, feet (ft.)
″	inch, inches (in.)

#	pound (lb.) or number
:	ratio or proportion ("is to")
°F	degrees in Fahrenheit
°C	degrees in centigrade

Appendix C

Abbreviations and Odd Words

ounce = oz.
gram = g
pound = lb.
kilogram = kg
liter = l
milliliter = ml
centimeter = cm
ton (tonne) = t
quart = qt.
inch = in. (also written as ″)
gallon = gal.
foot = ft. (singular)
feet = ft. (plural) (also written as ′)
kilometer = km

cup = c.
tablespoon = tbs or tbsp
teaspoon = tsp
yard = yd.
meter = m
mile or miles = mi.
miles per hour = mph
millimeter = mm
deciliter = dl
pint = pt.
decimeter = dm
kilometers per hour = kph
degrees Fahrenheit = °F
degrees centigrade = °C

Glossary

Abbreviation Short form; quick way to write something.

A bit less than Not quite as much; under; somewhat.

A bit more than Over, above, somewhat.

About Close to; nearly the same; almost.

Absolute value The relative value of something—how far, how much—without the minus sign.

Adapt Adjust, get used to, change.

Addition Add to; increase by; add; plus.

Afford The amount one can spend without "overspending"; manage; budget.

After tax Net income, take-home pay.

Almost Close to; nearly the same; not quite; approximately.

American Standard Measurement (ASM) This is the system used in the United States to measure distance, weight (mass), temperature, and volume (liquid and dry measures).

Apparent Obvious; plain; evident.

Application Use of; way to use something.

Apply for Look for (as in a job or apartment).

Approximately Nearly; close to; almost the same.

Approximating Estimating; coming close to; not exact.

ASM American Standard Measurement.

At ease Comfortable.

Before tax Pretax; gross income; total income.

Bill Amount to be paid, amount owed; charge; cost.

Bounce a check To write a check when there is not enough money in your checking account to pay the bill. This is illegal.

Bounced check A check that has been returned to you because there was not enough money in your checking account to pay it.

Brush up on Refresh; renew; remind.

Budget Spending plan.

Campground Caravan park.

Capital gains The growth in the value of a stock or a stock-based mutual fund.

Capital loss The decline in the value of a stock or a stock-based mutual fund.

CD Certificate of deposit.

Certificate of deposit A bank investment that pays a set (predetermined) amount of interest each month, quarter, half year, or year.

Charges Costs; bill; expenses.

Checking account A bank account that allows you to write checks to access (get to) your deposits of money. This is an easy (convenient) way to pay bills, buy things, and manage your money. Direct deposit allows your take-home pay to be sent directly to this checking account.

Close to Nearly the same; about; almost; similar.

Combine Add; add together; merge; mix; blend.

Comfortable At ease; familiar with; used to.

Component Element; part; portion; piece.

Compound fraction A fraction that is greater than 1 and has a whole-number component.

Comprehend Understand; know; follow.

Connection Relationship.

Conversion Change between two systems or languages.

Costs Bills; charges; expenses.

Cup A unit of measurement equal to 8 ounces (oz.); abbreviated c. or c (singular and plural).

Customs The way we do things, the "ins and outs" of a particular culture.

Decimal The portion of a number that is to the right of the period (decimal point).

Decrease Reduce; shorten.

Direct deposit A program that allows your employer to send your net (take-home) pay directly to your bank account. Usually this deposit is made to your checking account.

Dividend The "interest" paid on a stock or a stock-based mutual fund.

Early Too soon.

Earnings Pay; salary; hourly wage; income.

Earnings Statement The paperwork that comes with your paycheck. If you have direct deposit, this is all you will receive—your pay will go directly to your checking account.

Easier Simpler; more workable; more manageable.

Element Part; component.

English as a Second Language (ESL) The process or means of acquiring and using an additional language that is not one's first language.

Equation A mathematical operation that can be solved—it has an equal (=) sign.

Equivalent The same as, equal to, very close to the same value.

Error Mistake.

ESL English as a Second Language.

Estimating Approximating.

Exact Precise; same.

Expenses Costs; charges; bills.

Expression 1. A mathematical operation that does not have an equal (=) sign and does not have enough information to be solved. 2. A way of saying something; an idiom, phrase, or saying.

Fees Tolls; charges.

Feet The plural of foot abbreviated ft or ft.

Follow 1. Come after; come next. 2. Understand; read; comprehend; know.

Foot A unit of measurement equal to 12 inches; abbreviated ft or ft.

Fraction A number that is less than one.

Fuel Gas; gasoline; diesel.

Gallon Abbreviated gal. or gal (plural is gals.).

Gas, gasoline Fuel; diesel.

Get rid of Eliminate; drop.

Gross income Pretax income; income before paying taxes.

Hybrid Mixed; combined; compound.

Idiom The way things are said. The meaning may not relate to the meaning of each individual word. Phrases; jargon; sayings; expressions.

Inch A unit of measurement; 12 inches is 1 foot. Abbreviated in. or in or ″.

Increase Lengthen; expand; make longer.

Ins and outs Customs; how things are done in a culture.

Interest The earnings (as a percentage) on savings and some other investments (such as CDs or bonds).

Jargon Idiom; slang; expressions; sayings.

Know Follow; understand; recognize; comprehend.

Landlord The person you are renting an office, house, or apartment from.

Late Past due; overdue.

Lengthen Increase; make longer; expand.

Like Similar to; such as.

Liter A metric unit of volume equal to approximately 1.056 liquid quarts, 0.908 dry quart, or 0.264 gallon (from the online dictionary at www.websters.com).

Look up Find, locate.

Manage Plan; take care of; control.

Math Mathematics.

Meter The international standard unit of length, approximately equivalent to 39.37 inches. It was redefined in 1983 as the distance traveled by light in a vacuum in 1/299,792,458 of a second (from the online dictionary at www.websters.com).

Mile Abbreviated mi. or mi (singular and plural).

Minus Less than; take away; below zero; decrease; reduce; reduced; negative.

Mistake Error.

MPH, mph Miles per hour (singular and plural).

Near Close; similar.

Nearly Close to; approximately; about; almost.

Negative Less than zero.

Net income Income after taxes are taken out; after-tax income; take-home pay.

Observe See; notice.

Obvious Apparent.

Ounce Abbreviated oz. or oz (singular and plural).

Overdue Late; past due.

Part Component; element; piece.

Past due Late; overdue.

Pay Salary or hourly wage; earnings; income.

Phrases Expressions; sayings; idiom; jargon; slang.

Pint Abbreviated pt. or pt (plural is pts).

Plus More than; add to; above zero; increase; increased; positive; combine.

Positive Greater than zero.

Pound Abbreviated lb. or lb (plural is lbs.).

Practical mathematics Applied mathematics.

Precise Exact.

Pretax income Gross income; income before taxes are taken out; total income.

Previous Past; earlier.

Pronounce Say; speak.

Quart Abbreviated qt. or qt (plural is qts.).

Reduce Decrease; shorten.

Rounding Reducing (rounding down) or increasing (rounding up) the value of a number to make the number easier to add, subtract, multiply, or divide.

Sales tax A tax added when an item is purchased.

See Observe; notice.

Shorten Decrease; reduce.

Similar Close; near; approximate.

Simpler Easier; more manageable; workable.

Slang Idiom; jargon; sayings; expressions.

Subtraction Take away; reduce by; remove; minus.

Such as For example.

Suitable Correct; appropriate.

Tablespoon A unit of measurement equal to 3 teaspoons; abbreviated tbs or tbsp (singular and plural).

Take-home pay Income after taxes are taken out; net income; net pay.

Teaspoon A unit of measurement equal to 1/3 tablespoon; abbreviated tsp (singular and plural).

Tolls User fees.

Ton Same as tonne; abbreviated t or T (singular and plural).

Too soon Early.

Total return The amount an investment grows or declines: interest plus dividends plus capital gains or capital losses.

Understand Know; be familiar with; become familiar with; learn.

Use Apply.

Yard Abbreviated yd. or yd (plural is yds.).

About the Author

Janet C. Arrowood is a full-time writer and trainer and an adjunct professor of mathematics at several Denver-area colleges. She is the author of numerous reference books for insurance, educational, fire mitigation, and financial audiences, and is a regular contributor to a variety of legal, insurance, financial, and other publications.